AA

World of Discovery
Great Wonders

AA Publishing

Compiled by Ann F Stonehouse
Designed by Kat Mead

Produced by AA Publishing

© Automobile Association Developments Limited 2006
Relief maps created from originals supplied by Getty Images/The Studio Dog and
Mountain High Maps®, Copyright © 1993 Digital Wisdom

Published by AA Publishing (a trading name of Automobile Association Developments Limited,
whose registered office is Fanum House, Basing View, Basingstoke, Hampshire RG21 4EA.
Registered number 1878835).

Large format ISBN-10: 0-7495-4983-1
Large format ISBN-13: 978-0-7495-4983-1
Small format ISBN-10: 0-7495-5006-6
Small format ISBN-13: 978-0-7495-5006-6

A02893

The AA's website address is www.theAA.com/bookshop

A CIP catalogue record for this book is available from the British Library.

Origination by Keene Group, Andover
Printed and bound in China by Everbest Printing Co Ltd

World of Discovery
Great Wonders

Contents

+1   +2   +3   +4   +5   +6   +7   +8   +9   +10   +11   +12

Time Zone Map

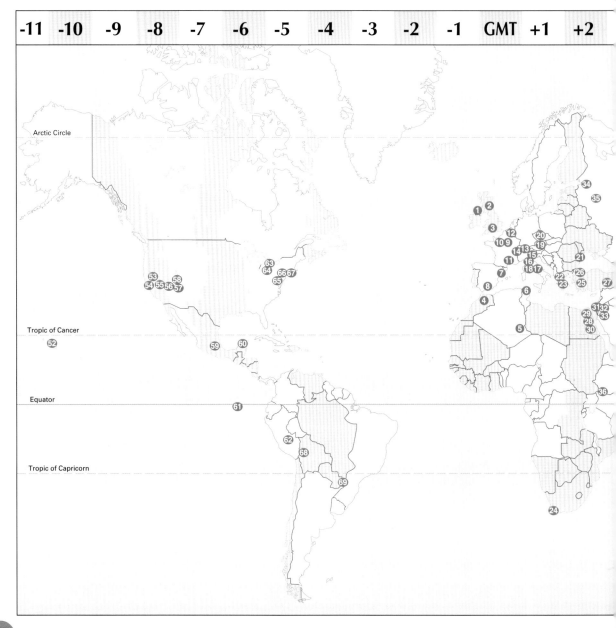

-11	-10	-9	-8	-7	-6	-5	-4	-3	-2	-1	GMT	+1	+2

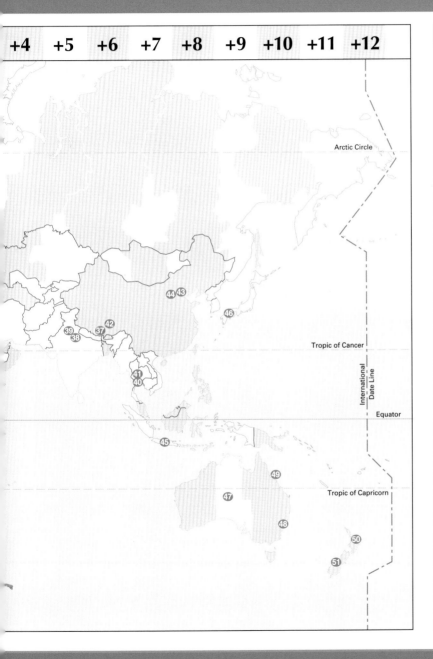

+4 +5 +6 +7 +8 +9 +10 +11 +12

Arctic Circle

Tropic of Cancer

Equator

International Date Line

Tropic of Capricorn

The wonders

1	Giant's Causeway	36	Rift Valley
2	Edinburgh Castle	37	The Himalayas
3	Stonehenge	38	Taj Mahal
4	Fez Medina	39	Red Fort
5	Sahara Desert	40	Wat Phra Kaew
6	Carthage	41	Ayutthaya
7	Sagrada Família	42	Potala Palace
8	Alhambra	43	Forbidden City
9	Eiffel Tower	44	Great Wall of China
10	Versailles	45	Borobudur
11	Pont du Gard	46	Itsukushima Shrine
12	Grand' Place	47	Uluru
13	Kapellbrücke	48	Sydney Opera House
14	The Matterhorn	49	Great Barrier Reef
15	Grand Canal	50	Rotorua
16	Leaning Tower of Pisa	51	Southern Alps
17	Colosseum	52	Hawaiian Islands
18	St. Peter's Basilica	53	Redwoods & Giant
19	Hofburg		Sequoias
20	Golden Lane	54	Golden Gate Bridge
21	Danube Delta	55	Yosemite National Park
22	Metéora Monasteries	56	Hoover Dam
23	Parthenon	57	Grand Canyon
24	Table Mountain	58	Zion National Park
25	Pamukkale	59	Teotihuacán
26	Blue Mosque	60	Chichén Itzá
27	Nemrut Dag	61	Galapagos Islands
28	River Nile	62	Machu Picchu
29	Great Pyramid	63	CN Tower
30	Temple of Karnak	64	Niagara Falls
31	Jerusalem	65	Lincoln Memorial
32	Dead Sea	66	Statue of Liberty
33	Petra	67	Empire State Building
34	Great Palace	68	Inca Trails
35	Kremlin	69	Iguassu Falls

What time is it where?

In 1884 the International Meridian Conference divided the world's 360 degrees of longitude into 15-degree time zones, one for each hour of the 24-hour day. As the zero degree line of longitude ran through Greenwich, Great Britain, basic time for the world was established as Greenwich Mean Time or GMT. Time east of Greenwich is ahead of GMT and time west of Greenwich behind.

Zones shown on the map are Standard Time; Summer Time or Daylight Saving Time, adopted by some countries for part of the year, is not shown.

Introduction

The Ancient World claimed just seven wonders—of which only the pyramids of Egypt survive. In this modern age of fast communication and visual imagery, the number of wonders we are all exposed to through superb photography have multiplied beyond anything which people in ancient times could possibly have predicted. We have a better knowledge of our world, its spectacular showpieces of nature, and our human achievements in it.

So what makes something a wonder? Indeed, is there anything left to wonder at, or has mass communication made us all blasé? The answer has to be a resounding "yes, there is"—because photos, however vivid, can neither replace the involuntary intake of breath when you see the beauty of the Taj Mahal for real, nor deafen your senses in the way that the thunderous, continuous roar of a mighty waterfall such as Niagara or Iguassu does.

Whatever makes you gasp with surprise, you'll find more about it in this fabulous collection. There are wonders from the ancient past, of course— ruined temples like Petra, with an air of mystery, where we try to imagine the civilizations that built them; and monuments such as Stonehenge, so majestic yet so old that their purpose has become lost in time. There are modern feats of engineering that perhaps changed the world when they were constructed—including the Empire State Building, and the Hoover Dam. There are palaces and structures so extravagant that your jaw drops when you read about them, such as Versailles and the Great Wall of China. And there are the awesome phenomena of nature before which so much seems so insignificant: the redwoods of California, the birdlife of the Danube Delta, and the shifting sands of the Sahara Desert.

Enjoy reading about these wonders and more in this beautifully illustrated book, make up your own top seven list as you go, and be inspired to go and see them for real.

Giant's Causeway

facts &
figures

- The Giant's Causeway is made up of about 40,000 tightly packed hexagonal basalt columns, which are up to 90 feet (27m) thick in some places.

- The tallest columns, seen in the cliffs, rise up to 40 feet (12m) above sea level.

- The columns were formed around 60 million years ago, when molten lava spewed up from the seabed.

myth &
music

- According to legend, the Giant's Causeway was created by giant Finn MacCool, who intended to fight his neighbor, Finn Gall, in Scotland.

- While Finn MacCool rested from his labors, Finn Gall sneaked across the causeway, but was so frightened at the sight of the sleeping giant that he ran home.

- The Scottish island of Staffa also has basalt columns, and inspired a Mendelssohn overture.

▶ A REMARKABLE NATURAL STONE WALKWAY STRETCHES OUT INTO THE WILD ATLANTIC SEA, OFF THE NORTH ANTRIM COASTLINE OF NORTHERN IRELAND.

did **you** know?

...it's here?

TIME ZONE: GIANT'S CAUSEWAY GMT

Eire

Ireland

? Another great place to see columnar basalt is at the waterfall of Svartifoss, in Skaftafell, Iceland.

Q *What was the name of Felix Mendelssohn's overture?*

A The Hebrides.

► When it is midday at the Giant's Causeway it is 9am in Brasília and 2pm at the Great Pyramid...   ...do you know where they are?

Edinburgh Castle

stronghold &
fortress

- The castle is built on a high ridge of basalt, with the Old Town of Edinburgh extending down the ridge to Holyrood Palace.

- There's been a castle on this site since the Iron Age, but the oldest building there now is the 11th-century St. Margaret's Chapel.

- Around 1 million visitors walk through the castle gateway every year to admire the ancient buildings resonant with Scottish history, and to enjoy spectacular views of the city below.

► THE MAJESTIC CASTLE, DATING BACK TO MEDIEVAL TIMES DOMINATES THE SKYLINE OF SCOTLAND'S HISTORIC AND BEAUTIFUL CAPITAL CITY.

did **you** know?

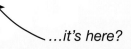

...it's here?

Alba

treasury &
prison

- The Scottish crown, part of the Scottish Regalia held in the castle, dates from 1540 and is made of Scottish gold.

- During wars in the 18th and 19th centuries, French prisoners were held here, and the graffiti they etched into the walls can still be seen.

Edinburgh Castle *Scotland*

Q *Which event, which is watched on TV by 100 million viewers around the world, takes place on the Castle Esplanade in summer?*

A *The Military Tattoo.*

13

Stonehenge

facts &
figures

- Some of the huge standing stones in this ancient henge are 25 feet (8m) high, and weigh up to 40 tons.

- The bluestones which lie within the outer sandstone ring are thought to have been transported all the way from Preseli in South Wales, perhaps partly by water.

- Up to 4,500 visitors a day come to the site.

▶ A RING OF STONES, RAISED SOME 5,000 YEARS AGO ON A LEVEL PLAIN IN SOUTHERN ENGLAND, IS EUROPE'S MOST IMPORTANT PREHISTORIC MONUMENT.

did **you** know?

...it's here?

England

history & **mystery**

- Stonehenge was constructed in phases over many years, but the first circular ditch and mound date to 3100BC.

- The massive sandstone blocks topped with lintels were added around 2100BC.

- The axis of the inner stones and an ancient approach road are both aligned with the midsummer sun, suggesting that this may have been a prehistoric astronomical observatory—but nobody knows this for sure.

Q *Which other famous stone circle lies close to Stonehenge?*

A *Avebury.*

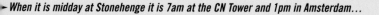

► When it is midday at Stonehenge it is 7am at the CN Tower and 1pm in Amsterdam...   ...do you know where they are?

15

Fez Medina

scale &
history

- The Medina at Fez, also known by the name Fez el Bali, dates from an age when the city was a key center of academic debate—it has one of the oldest universities in the world.

- The old city was divided into around 200 districts, each a community in its own right complete with mosque, bath house, and bakery.

- The city was established in the 9th century. By the 13th century it had thousands of shops and nearly 800 mosques (with schools attached).

- The most famous buildings in the winding streets of the old quarter include 13th-century Karouyine Mosque (the largest in North Africa), and the Bou Inania Medrassah—a Koran school arranged around a courtyard.

- Traditional skills are still practised in the Medina, including tanning, and dyeing of cloth in clay pits. The dyers have their own *souk* (marketplace) by the river, and a watermill to crush the seeds that provide color for the dyes.

> ▶ FEZ MEDINA IS THE PRESERVED MEDIEVAL SECTOR OF FEZ, A MODERN MOROCCAN CITY WITH MORE THAN HALF A MILLION INHABITANTS.

did **you** know?

←_____ ...it's here?

 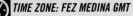

Fez Medina *Morocco*

Q Where does the name Medina originate?

A It was the city to which the Prophet Muhammed escaped in AD622, and is now applied to the old part of any Islamic city.

➤ When it is midday at Fez Medina it is 3pm in Baghdad and 8pm in the Forbidden City... ...do you know where they are?

Sahara Desert

sand &
more sand

- The Sahara covers an area of almost 3.6 million square miles (9.3 million sq km), stretching from Egypt and the Sudan to the west coasts of Mauretania and Spanish Sahara.

- A sea of baking golden sand, it also has areas of barren, rocky terrain, and parched scrubland.

- Kebili is one of the hottest places in the Sahara, where daytime temperatures can soar to an incredible 131°F (55°C). Yet at night, after the sun has gone down, temperatures here may drop below freezing point.

- The Sirocco wind fuels the high temperatures caused by the sun. This wind originates in the interior of the Sahara, and funnels hot air northwards like a mighty furnace blast.

- Nomadic tribes still wander the Sahara with their small herds of beasts; the people who wear the distinctive indigo-blue robes are generally from the western and central parts.

? The rolling Sahara sands can be highly mobile, with dunes driven by the wind shifting up to 36 feet (11m) a year.

▶ THE GREAT SAHARA IN NORTH AFRICA IS THE LARGEST DESERT IN THE WORLD. IT IS AN EVER-GROWING ARID EXPANSE WHERE HIDDEN LIFE SURVIVES, DESPITE THE HARDSHIPS.

did **you** know?

...it's here?

North Africa

Q What are the green areas that grow up around waterholes called?

A Oases.

► When it is midday in the Sahara Desert it is 1pm at the Grand Canal and 5pm in Karachi...   ...do you know where they are?

Carthage

? Some of the oldest archaeological finds in Carthage suggest the city once had a sinister tradition of sacrificing children to the deity Baal Hammon.

▶ THE EXTENSIVE RUINS OF WHAT WAS ONCE A SPECTACULAR CITY ON THE COAST OF NORTH AFRICA TELL AN INTRIGUING TALE OF POWER, LOVE, AND EVENTUAL DESTRUCTION.

did **you** know?

...it's here?

Tunisia

الجمهورية التونسية

Carthage *Tunisia*

powerful & **threatening**

- The city, a major naval port, was founded around the end of the ninth century BC, and grew to be a major power over the following 300 years.

- The Carthaginians threatened the supremacy of the Roman Empire, and conflict between the two powers became increasingly bloody.

- In 149BC the city was finally besieged by the Roman army, and reduced to ruins in a fire that lasted for ten days.

epic & **romantic**

- Carthage was founded by Queen Dido, who came here after her brother murdered her husband.

- Virgil's epic poem, *The Aeneid,* tells how the Trojan prince Aeneas arrived here on his way to Italy after defeat at Troy, and Dido fell in love with him.

- The legend poignantly continues that after Aeneas left, the Queen, in her grief, committed suicide.

➤ *When it is midday at Carthage it is 6am at the Statue of Liberty and 1pm in Oslo...* *...do you know where they are?*

Sagrada Família
España
Spain

▶ THE MASTERPIECE OF ARTIST ANTONI GAUDÍ REMAINS UNFINISHED TO THIS DAY, THE MOST FAMOUS LANDMARK IN HIS ADOPTED CITY OF BARCELONA.

did **you** know?

...it's here?

TIME ZONE: SAGRADA FAMÍLIA GMT+1

Q *Antoni Gaudí, the designer of the Sagrada Família, died how, in 1926?*

A *He was run over by a tram.*

23

▶ **When it is midday at the Sagrada Família it is 1pm at the Dead Sea and 7pm in Kuala Lumpur...** *...do you know where they are?*

Q *What unusual technique did Gaudí employ to sculpt the donkey for the Nativity facade?*

A *He took plaster casts of a real donkey.*

inspiration &
beginnings

- Antoni Gaudí was born in 1852 in Reus, Spain, the son of a coppersmith, and became one of the country's most famous artists.

- His work has become a defining feature of Barcelona, and can be seen across the city in weirdly sculptural buildings and idiosyncratic features, and the exuberant ceramic-tiled forms of Güell Park.

- He was commissioned to design and build a great basilica, the Sagrada Família (the Church of the Holy Family), and work started in 1884.

- Gaudí worked to rough sketches rather than fixed and detailed plans, and prefered to supervise and adapt the work on site.

- After his death, with no clear legacy of details or blueprints to show how the church should be completed, it remained unfinished, and controversy about attempts to complete it still rage to this day.

organic &
unusual

- The 12 towers of the facades represent the Apostles, and Gaudí planned another six which would represent Christ, the Virgin, and the Evangelists.

- Three monumental facades were planned, to depict the Nativity, the Passion, and the Resurrection, and each would be topped by huge towers.

- The towers of the original and almost surreal Nativity facade were completed in the 1950s.

- An entirely new Passion facade obscures some of Gaudí's original design.

- Gaudí was inspired by the colors and forms of nature, and a glimpse of his other buildings in Barcelona, including Casa Milá and Casa Batlló, suggest the stonework of the church would not have been left in its original shades.

Alhambra

stronghold & **paradise**

- The Alhambra was built by the Moors in the 13th century as a fortress, and was designed to defend the occupying Islamic powers from a possible Christian resurgence.

- It was begun on the orders of Muhammad I al Ghalib, founder of the Muslim Nasrid dynasty—the last Muslim ruler of Granada who was driven into exile in 1492.

- Within the walls of the Alhambra are gardens, courtyards, and a variety of apartments sumptuously decorated with ceramic tiles, pierced stonework, carved foliage designs and elaborate calligraphy that make it appear a true paradise on earth.

- Evocatively named sections include the Court of Myrtles, where the trees are planted in beds beside a long pool, and the Court of the Lions, where a fountain is supported by 12 stone lions. The Hall of the Ambassadors, where royal audiences were held, has a carved ceiling 60 feet (18m) high to suggest the heavens.

▶ MOORISH INFLUENCES ARE SEEN AT THEIR BEST IN THIS FABULOUS ROYAL PALACE AND GARDEN AT GRANADA, IN SOUTHERN SPAIN.

did **you** know?

...it's here?

España

Q *Where did the Moors originate?*

Alhambra *Spain*

A North Africa.

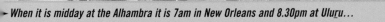

➤ **When it is midday at the Alhambra it is 7am in New Orleans and 8.30pm at Uluru...**   *...do you know where they are?*

27

Eiffel Tower

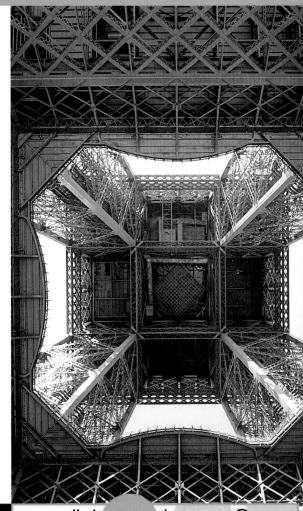

industrial &
artistic

- The slender grace and strength of this famous structure symbolize the achievements of the industrial age in the late 19th century.

- The Tower was the brainchild of engineer Gustav Eiffel (1832–1923), who was challenged to create a structure that would stand over 1,000 feet (300m) high as the centerpiece for the Paris Exposition of 1889.

- From the start, the tower was used to support scientific research, holding meteorological equipment to measure weather at high altitudes, and later radio and television aerials.

- Eiffel's ingenious use of filigree ironwork reduced the surface area of the tower to a minimum, enhancing its ability to withstand environmental stresses such as windforce.

- Not everybody approved of the tower when it was first built, fearing that it detracted from the city's classical skyline, or that it might collapse and cause widespread destruction.

▶ FOR MORE THAN 100 YEARS THE EIFFEL TOWER HAS BEEN THE SYNONYMOUS SYMBOL OF PARIS, ITS DISTINCTIVE SILHOUETTE RECOGNIZED ACROSS THE WORLD.

did **you** know?

...it's here?

France

? There are **1,665** steps to the top of the tower—but visitors can now take an elevator ride to the top from the second floor.

Eiffel Tower *France*

29

Versailles

? In selecting Versailles as the location for his grand palace, Louis turned his back on established palaces within Paris including the Louvre and the Tuileries.

▶ LOUIS XIV PLANNED A CHATEAU JUST OUTSIDE PARIS THAT WOULD ACCOMMODATE THE WHOLE COURT AND SHOW FRENCH STYLE AND MAGNIFICENCE TO THE WORLD.

did **you** know?

...it's here?

France

grandeur & **excess**

- Louis XIV, "the Sun King", transformed the site of a modest former hunting lodge, to create one of the grandest, most opulent palaces the world had ever seen. His successors added to its splendor until they were cut short by the French Revolution in 1789.

- The palace was started in 1661, and the money spent on its lavish creation almost brought the French treasury to its knees.

- The garden frontage of the palace extends for 2,100 feet (640m), and the fabulous Salle des Glaces (Hall of Mirrors) gallery inside is 235 feet (72m) long, with a painted ceiling 42 feet (12.8m) high and 17 vast windows down one side that are matched by mirrors on the opposite wall.

- The gardens, planned and laid out by the great André Le Nôtre, cover around 250 acres (101ha), and hold a wealth of monumental sculptures.

Q *Which notorious queen built a rustic hamlet in the grounds and played at being a shepherdess?*

A *Marie-Antoinette.*

Pont du Gard

practical &
purposeful

- The Pont du Gard looks like an unusually grand three-tiered bridge, but in fact its primary purpose was as an aqueduct.

- It was built by the Romans around 19BC as part of a watercourse that stretched all the way from Uzés, 30 miles (48km) to Nîmes, bringing fresh water to that great Roman city.

- The aqueduct spans the River Gordon, and is 160 feet (49m) high and 900 feet (247m) long.

- Despite their regular appearance, the arches in each tier are not, in fact, identical.

Q *Who was responsible for the building of the Pont du Gard?*

A *The Roman pro-consul Agrippa (c.63–12BC).*

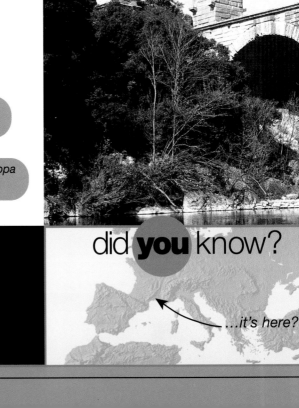

▶ THE PONT DU GARD, A SUPERB, SOARING STRUCTURE NEAR THE CITY OF NÎMES IN SOUTHERN FRANCE, IS A REMARKABLE SURVIVOR OF AN EARLIER AGE.

did **you** know?

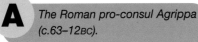

...it's here?

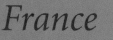

construction &
maintenance

- The Pont du Gard has three tiers of arches, with 6 at the bottom, 11 in the middle, and 35 along the top.

- The top arches support the water channel, which was required to bring water to Nîmes not only for drinking, but also to supply the town's many ornamental fountains. Pedestrians used to be able to walk across this top row of arches, but in recent years it has become dangerous to do so.

- The stone blocks of the aqueduct were cut precisely to fit, and laid without the use of mortar, making this a remarkable survivor of the mason's skill.

- Stone knobs protruding from the otherwise smooth surface of the aqueduct were used to support scaffolding, which would have been essential for regular maintenance work.

- Today a modern bridge runs closely alongside the aqueduct, echoing its lower arches perfectly, and allowing the best close-up views.

- A modern visitor center nearby tells the full story of the building of the structure and its remarkable survival.

- When it is midday at the Pont du Gard it is 11am in Edinburgh and 7pm at the Great Wall of China...   ...do you know where they are?

Grand' Place

growth & **destruction**

- The Hôtel de Ville (Town Hall), the first major building on the square, dates from around 1402 and occupies most of one side.

- This splendid building is dominated by its spire, a dizzying 300 feet (91m) high, and designed some 50 years later by the architect Jan van Ruysbroek.

- The facade of the Hôtel de Ville is adorned with more than 100 statues—the original versions of these were replaced by copies during the 19th century.

- In 1695 the French army bombarded the city for 36 hours, causing the destruction of 16 churches and many thousands of houses in the city, as well as the original wooden guild houses that surrounded Grand' Place.

- What you see today was therefore largely constructed after this date, and was built to survive in stone.

renaissance & **rebuilding**

- It is no surprise that the phoenix—the mythical beast which rose again out of the flames—is the symbol of the city. Look for one on the end gable of La Louve, a guild house that belonged to the Guild of Archers.

- The buildings around Grand' Place were reconstructed in stone to survive the centuries. They are in a flamboyant baroque style with pinnacles, curlicues, statues, gargoyles, medallions, and heraldic beasts.

- The Maison du Roi, opposite the Hôtel de Ville, was once the guildhall of the city's bakers, and was rebuilt at the end of the 19th century in 16th-century style.

- Today, the square is filled every day with a colorful flower market, and with the songs of caged birds on a Sunday morning.

▶ GRAND' PLACE IS THE LARGE CENTRAL SQUARE AT THE HEART OF THE BELGIAN CAPITAL, BRUSSELS, SURROUNDED BY A RICH HERITAGE OF HISTORIC BUILDINGS.

did **you** know?

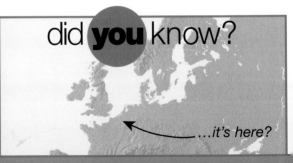

...it's here?

Belgique

When it is midday at the Grand' Place it is 7am in Caracas and 2pm at the Kremlin…   …do you know where they are?

Kapellbrücke

? The name Lucerne comes from *lucerna*, meaning lighthouse, and it is possible that there was once a lighthouse in the water tower on the bridge.

► EUROPE'S MOST VENERABLE WOODEN BRIDGE IS TO BE FOUND IN LUCERNE, SWITZERLAND, AT THE NORTHWEST CORNER OF LAKE LUCERNE.

did **you** know?

...it's here?

TIME ZONE: KAPELLBRÜCKE GMT+1

structure &
style

- Lucerne's Kapellbrücke (Chapel Bridge) was built in 1333, and is a covered wooden bridge that stretches for around 650 feet (198m) across the flowing Reuss River.

- Badly damaged by fire in 1993, it has since been fully restored.

- The bridge's primary purpose was defensive, and its building coincided with the construction of the city's defensive walls. At that time, Lucerne was part of the Swiss Confederation, a break-away group from the Holy Roman Empire and an early forerunner of what would later emerge as the independent nation of Switzerland.

- Seen from the river bank, its most notable feature is the octagonal, stone-built water tower, which has served at different times as a prison, a torture chamber, and even as the city's treasury.

- On the bridge itself, however, you can see its real highlight—112 paintings high in the wooden rafters, depicting key events in Lucerne's history and the struggle for Swiss independence. The paintings also show events in the lives of the city's two patron saints, St. Léger and St. Maurice.

Q *Which great composer wrote part of his famous* Ring Cycle *of operas while living just outside Lucerne?*

A *Richard Wagner (1813–83).*

When it is midday at the Kapellbrücke it is 1pm at the Danube Delta and 8pm in Tokyo...   ...do you know where they are?

37

The Matterhorn

▶ TOWERING ABOVE THE BORDER BETWEEN ITALY AND SWITZERLAND, THE DISTINCTIVE POINTED PEAK OF THE MATTERHORN IS A HIGHLIGHT OF THE ALPS.

did **you** know?

...it's here?

pointed &
rock-hard

- The Matterhorn is a pyramidal peak, with four steep faces converging on a narrow point, and is part of a mountain range ground out by ice around 2 million years ago.

- The mountain's core contains hard rocks such as granite, mica schist, and gneiss, with softer rocks such as sandstone and shales to be found at the edges.

steep &
deadly

- One of the world's most frequently scaled mountains, the Matterhorn is also one of the most deadly, even to experienced and expert climbers.

- The first team to reach the top was led by Englishman Edward Whymper, in 1865. Sadly three members of the team fell to their death as they made their descent from the mountain.

Q *The Matterhorn is not the highest of the Alps—do you know which mountain is?*

A *Mont Blanc, in France.*

When it is midday on the Matterhorn it is 1am in the Hawaiian islands and 6pm in Bangkok...   *...do you know where they are?*

Grand Canal

bustle &
architecture

- The Grand Canal snakes in a broad S-shape through the heart of Venice, from the train station in the northwest of the city to the Punta della Salute in the southeast—a distance of around 2.5 miles (4km).

- Traditional black gondolas and bustling *vaporetti* (motorized water-taxis) form the bulk of the canal's steady flow of traffic, filling the waterway with life and color at the height of the tourist season.

- The Grand Canal is lined with superb buildings that reflect a period of Venetian grandeur from the 13th century to the 20th. The monuments, palaces, mansions, and churches are constructed on wooden piles, lapped by the sea. Highlights include the 16th-century Ca' d'Oro, and the Palazzo Dario.

- Three bridges cross the canal. The oldest of these is the famous Ponte Rialto.

▶ THE GRAND CANAL IS THE MAIN ARTERY AND THOROUGHFARE OF THE MAGNIFICENT WATER-BOUND ITALIAN CITY OF VENICE.

did **you** know?

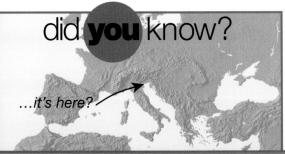

...it's here?

TIME ZONE: GRAND CANAL GMT+1

Q *Which famous square on the Grand Canal did Napoleon refer to as "the finest drawing room in Europe?"*

A St. Mark's Square.

At midday on the Grand Canal it is 11am in Reykjavík and 2pm at the Great Palace...   *...do you know where they are?*

Leaning Tower of Pisa

construction & subsidence

- The Leaning Tower, known in Italian as the Torre Pendente, is part of a complex of fine buildings in the heart of Pisa, and an error by its architects has made it the most famous of the group.

- It was built in 1173 as the belltower, or *campanile*, of the cathedral nearby, which had been started around 100 years earlier.

- It appears that the ground beneath the tower was less than solid, and the structure began to lean very early in its history—not exactly helped by the top-heavy addition of the seventh level in around 1360.

- Efforts in the 20th century to stabilize the Leaning Tower succeeded in pulling it back by about half a degree, but it remains about 15 feet (4.6m) out of perpendicular.

▶ PISA'S EXTRAORDINARY LEANING TOWER, DESIGNED TO HOLD THE BELLS OF THE NEIGHBORING CATHEDRAL, IS ONE OF THE WONDERS OF ITALY.

did **you** know?

...it's here?

Italia

Q *Which famous scientist, born in Pisa, dropped a variety of objects from the Leaning Tower to prove his theories of gravity?*

A Galileo Galilei (1564–1642).

At midday at the Leaning Tower of Pisa it is 6am in Toronto and 11am at the Giant's Causeway... ...do you know where they are?

43

Colosseum

Q From which rival civilization did the Romans borrow the design of the amphitheater?

A The Greeks.

▶ THE COLOSSEUM, WHICH LOOMS OVER 180 FEET (55M) HIGH IN THE HEART OF ITALY'S CAPITAL CITY, ROME, IS A REMARKABLE SURVIVOR OF A BLOODTHIRSTY AGE.

did **you** know?

...it's here?

Italia

history &
architecture

- After a fire swept through Rome in AD64, the Emperor Vespasian ordered the biggest and best arena to be built and named it after his family— the Flavian Amphitheater.

- The new arena was opened by Vespasian's successor, Emperor Titus, in AD80.

- The Colosseum (a name it was given in the 8th century) was built of travertine stone, tufa, and brick, and could seat up to 50,000 spectators. A vast awning could be stretched over the open top of the amphitheater, with pulleys and ropes operated by sailors.

lions &
Christians

- Gladiatorial contests between professional fighters, and combats against a variety of animals such as stags, lions, and even ostriches, were the staple entertainment on offer.

- The Colosseum became Church property in the 13th century, and in 1744 it was consecrated in memory of the Christians said to have died for their faith in front of the baying Romans.

- Despite this, there is little real evidence of Christian martyrdom on the site.

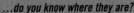

⟶ At midday at the Colosseum it is 8am in Buenos Aires and 1pm on Table Mountain...   *...do you know where they are?*

St. Peter's Basilica

▶ ROME'S MASSIVE CATHEDRAL, IN THE PAPAL HOME OF THE VATICAN, IS RECOGNIZED ACROSS THE WORLD AS THE SPIRITUAL HEART OF ROMAN CATHOLICISM.

did **you** know?

...it's here?

Stato della Città del Vaticano

statistics &
history

- St. Peter's covers a staggering area of 240,000 square feet (22,296 sq m), with a dome 453 feet (138m) high and 138 feet (42m) in diameter.

- It is built over the tomb of St. Peter, who was crucified by the Roman emperor Nero around AD64, and it is a major site of pilgrimage.

- The cathedral was started in the 16th century, but the huge square in front of it, with its colonnade of 284 Tuscan pillars, dates from the 17th century.

- The interior of the basilica is elaborately and rather heavily decorated, and includes works of art such as Bernini's bronze High Altar canopy, and Michelangelo's exquisite *Pietà*. This is a marble statue of the Virgin Mary holding the lifeless body of Jesus Christ.

- St. Peter's stands in the tiny autonomous Vatican City state, which has the Pope at its head and includes famous buildings such as the Sistine Chapel.

Q *Who designed the bright, striped uniform worn by the papal guards?*

A *The artist Michelangelo (1475–1564).*

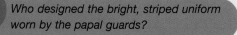

Hofburg

▶ The mighty Hofburg palace in Vienna was the imperial seat of Austria's glittering Hapsburg dynasty until 1918.

did **you** know?

...it's here?

Österreich

imposing &
imperial

- The Hofburg is a sprawling complex of buildings ranging in date from the 13th to the 19th centuries, and became the regular royal residence after 1533, when the emperor Ferdinand I made it his permanent home.

- The Hapsburgs amassed various imperial collections which are displayed here today, including one of musical instruments—appropriate to such a famously musical city.

royal court &
riding school

- Also on display in the palace are the treasury, with the gem-studded 10th-century imperial crown and a notable holy relic, and the gymnasium where Elisabeth, wife of the last emperor, Franz Josef, kept fit.

- The Spanish Riding School, known around the world for the aristocratic riding displays given by its stately white Lipizzaner horses, trained for war, is also part of the complex.

- The Augustinerkirche is the royal court's parish church, where hearts of the Hapsburg elite are interred, and where the unfortunate Marie-Antoinette married the future Louis XVI of France—both would lose their heads in the French Revolution.

- Vienna is a city which is famous worldwide for its music. Many great composers lived and worked here including Mozart (1756–91) and Christoph Gluck (1714–87) who wrote operas for the Hapsburg Court.

- Emperor Franz Josef, who died in 1916 after a reign of almost 80 years, had a rather plain bedroom here.

Golden Lane

simple &
mysterious

- Golden Lane is a narrow, cobblestone street lined with small, pastel-painted houses with diminutive doors and windows, low roofs, and a cluster of chimneys, built tightly against the looming palace wall.

- In the 16th century these modest little houses were occupied by the castle's guards, and later the street was taken over by goldsmiths.

- Its previous name was The Street of the Alchemists—alchemists could reputedly turn base metal into gold.

- Today it is one of Prague's top tourist attractions, and the little houses are occupied by cafés and souvenir shops, bringing in their own sort of gold.

- Golden Lane is officially part of the castle complex—once the home of the rulers of Bohemia, and more recently the official residence of the Czech president.

▶ THE BEST-KNOWN STREET IN THE CZECH REPUBLIC IS A LANE OF QUAINT LITTLE HOUSES, FOUND IN THE SHADOW OF PRAGUE'S HRADCANY CASTLE.

did you know?

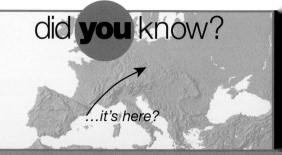

...it's here?

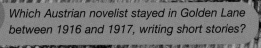

Q *Which Austrian novelist stayed in Golden Lane between 1916 and 1917, writing short stories?*

A *Franz Kafka (1883–1924).*

- At midday in Golden Lane it is 5am in Teotihuacán and 9pm in Beijing…   *…do you know where they are?*

Danube Delta

wet &
wild

- The Danube Delta, straddling the border between Romania and the Ukraine, covers an area of 2,317 square miles (6,000 sq km) at the point where the River Danube finishes its journey of 1,716 miles (2,761km) from the Black Forest in Germany.

- More than 300 different bird species have been recorded here, with about 180 species choosing to breed in the area while the others are migrants from as far afield as China, the Arctic, Siberia, and the Mediterranean.

- Four key species are the pygmy cormorant, the very rare, silvery-white Dalmatian pelican, the more familiar white pelican, and the red-breasted goose, whose entire population overwinters here.

- The waters of the delta and the nearby coastal waters support a large number of fish species, such as carp and sturgeon, making them increasingly vulnerable to human exploitation.

 The Danube is the second longest river in Europe after the Volga.

▶ CREATED AT THE POINT WHERE THE MIGHTY RIVER DANUBE MEETS THE BLACK SEA, A VAST WETLAND AREA IS A PARADISE FOR HUGE NUMBERS OF BIRDS.

did **you** know?

...it's here?

România

Q *Who composed the famous waltz tune, The Blue Danube, in 1867?*

A *Johann Strauss, the Younger (1825–99).*

- At midday on the Danube Delta it is 5am in Lima and 11am at the Alhambra...　　　　　*...do you know where they are?*

Metéora Monasteries

high &
precipitous

- Metéora means "in the air," and these monasteries are certainly as close to the sky as they can get, perched on rocky pinnacles up to 1,800 feet (549m) above the ground.

- They are located on the edge of the Pindus Mountains, overlooking the Pinios Valley.

isolated &
inaccessible

- There is a great tradition of Christian ascetics hiding themselves away in high places—in this case, it was Greek Orthodox monks, who first settled here around 1350.

- Until well into the 20th century, visitors had to climb up rickety ladders fastened to the rock, or perhaps be hauled up by hand in a basket.

▶ LOCATED NEAR KALABÁKA IN THESSALY, CENTRAL GREECE, THESE HISTORIC MONASTERIES ARE IMPOSSIBLY PERCHED ON THE TOP OF ROCK PINNACLES.

did you know?

...it's here?

Ελλάδα

disturbed &
deserted

- Adventurous visitors first spread the word of these monastic eyries in the 19th century, and after the 1960s visitor numbers increased after the building of a new access road.

- Now, many monks have moved away to regain their privacy, and the tiny communities are more like museum pieces.

 Life in a Metéora monastery was cramped, with little more than a few tiny cells, a church, and a refectory, and a cistern cut into the rock to collect vital rainwater.

At midday at the Metéora Monasteries it is 10am in Lisbon and 7pm at the Itsukushima Shrine…   …do you know where they are?

Parthenon

▶ THE PARTHENON IS THE CROWNING GLORY OF ATHENS, A SIGHT VISIBLE FROM ALL PARTS OF THE CITY AND A REMINDER OF A RICH HISTORY.

did you know?

...it's here?

TIME ZONE: PARTHENON GMT+2

Ελλάδα

Q Where can parts of the original stone frieze be seen preserved today?

A The British Museum in London.

classical & multi-purpose

- The Parthenon stands on the Acropolis, the site of an ancient city on a hilltop overlooking modern Athens.

- It was built in the mid-5th century BC as a temple to the goddess Athena, in the Doric style, and stands 228 feet (70m) long and 100 feet (31m) wide.

- The outer colonnade (or peristyle) enclosed an inner building, with a shrine and huge statue of the goddess. The colonnade is made up of 46 fluted marble pillars.

- The architect was a Greek man named Iktinos, who designed the structure to appear perfectly proportioned when viewed from below.

- The temple originally had a wooden roof, and stone-carved friezes ran around the walls of the inner building. These are believed to have shown an annual procession to present new robes to the statue of Athena.

- The Parthenon has had many other uses over the centuries, serving as both Greek Orthodox and Roman Catholic churches, and as a mosque. In the late 17th century Turkish forces used it as a gunpowder store—until it was blown up.

When it is midday at the Parthenon it is 5am at the Empire State Building and 1pm in Khartoum...   ...do you know where they are?

57

Table Mountain

? Cape Town was founded as a Dutch colony in 1652, to supply passing ships with fresh vegetables.

Q *Which three great oceans meet at this southern tip of South Africa?*

A *The Atlantic, Indian, and Southern oceans.*

▶ TABLE MOUNTAIN LOOMS HIGH OVER CAPE TOWN BAY, ITS FLAT TOP A FAMILIAR SIGHT TO SAILORS OF THE SOUTHERN SEAS.

did **you** know?

...it's here?

South Africa

shapely & **spectacular**

- Table Mountain stands around 3,500 feet (1,067m) above sea level, the flat top from which it takes its name stretching for 2 miles (3.2km) end to end.

- It is part of a range of hills that are made up of sandstone and quartzite, resting on shale and older rocks of granite.

- The mountain is the northern end of a range of hills that lies between Cape Town and the Cape of Good Hope, on the southern tip of South Africa.

- Rainfall on the mountaintop is around three times as high as that in the city which it shelters. The summit is often obscured by a blanket of white cloud known—of course—as "the tablecloth."

Table Mountain *South Africa*

- When it is midday on Table Mountain it is 11am at the Eiffel Tower and 4pm in Dhaka…   *…do you know where they are?*

Pamukkale

geothermal &
mineral-rich

- At Pamukkale the hot mineral springs bubble out of the ground near the top of a hill, emerging at a steaming temperature of about 109°F (43°C).

- The water, rich in calcium bicarbonate, evaporates steadily as it flows down the hill, leaving behind a veneer of snowy-white salt crystals called travertine.

- Over thousands of years, these mineral deposits have built up to form shallow natural basins. Tier upon tier may be seen on the hillside, the collected water in them reflecting sunlight and creating an extraordinary spectacle of nature.

- The Romans were perhaps the first to exploit these thermal pools, and today a modern spa on the site takes full advantage of the natural mineral-rich hot water.

- The thermal springs lie on a natural fault in the earth's crust, and there is seismic activity in this area almost every day.

Q What does the name Pamukkale mean?

A It's Turkish for "cotton castle."

> HOT SPRINGS IN A REMOTE CORNER OF WESTERN TURKEY HAVE GRADUALLY CREATED A DAZZLING, CASCADING TERRACE OF REFLECTIVE POOLS.

did **you** know?

...it's here?

Türkiye

When it is midday at Pamukkale it is 6am at La Paz and 1pm at the Rift Valley…   *…do you know where they are?*

Blue Mosque

Opposite the Blue Mosque stands another famous landmark, the domed basilica of Hagia Sofia—the Church of the Holy Wisdom.

▶ A VISIT TO THE WONDROUS BLUE MOSQUE IS A HIGHLIGHT OF ANY EXPLORATION OF THE GREAT TURKISH CITY OF ISTANBUL.

did **you** know?

...it's here?

TIME ZONE: BLUE MOSQUE GMT+2

Türkiye

design & **structure**

- The roofscape includes a central dome as well as 30 smaller ones.

- A distinctive feature is the minarets, which number an unusual six: one at each corner, plus two, slightly shorter towers, at the edge of the inner courtyard.

- The main interior structure of the Blue Mosque rests on four huge, elephant-foot columns, and is lit by the sunlight that floods in through 260 brilliant stained-glass windows.

- The mosque's Imperial Pavilion, where sultans would rest, now displays a fabulous museum collection of carpets and kilims.

construction & **detailing**

- The Blue Mosque was built in 1609 at the behest of the 19-year-old Sultan Ahmet I, the patron after whom it is officially named.

- Around 20,000 ceramic tiles, patterned in blue and other colors and manufactured in Iznik, were used to decorate the lavish interior of the mosque, to stunning effect.

- The floor is covered in thick carpets of deepest red, and both the *mimber* (pulpit) and the *mihrab* (the niche facing towards Mecca) are carved from gleaming white marble.

When it is midday at the Blue Mosque it is 10am at Stonehenge and 6pm in Singapore...   ...do you know where they are?

63

Nemrut Dag

lost & found

- The sculptures on the top of Nemrut Dag were created during the first century BC, in an area known as the Commagene that was ruled over by Antiochus I, a king of mixed Persian and Greek descent.

- After centuries of obscurity, the site was rediscovered by a German engineer, Karl Sester, in 1881.

- Sester found a tumulus, or burial mound, of loose stones on the mountaintop, which stood up to 160 feet (49m) high and 500 feet (152m) in diameter.

- The tumulus was guarded by the stone-carved figures of lions and eagles, and by broken, seated statues of Heracles (Hercules), Tyche, Zeus-Oromasdes, Apollo-Mithras, and King Antiochus himself.

- A similar, but less grand structure, belonging to Antiochus's father Mithridates I, was also found on nearby Nymphaios.

high & mighty

- The summit of Nemrut Dag, once part of Anatolia and now part of Turkey, stands 7,000 feet (2,134m) high.

- The statues were designed on a colossal scale, and stood about 30 feet (9m) tall when complete—all had lost their somewhat gnomic heads, which lay nearby.

- The style of carving on the heads reveals Greek facial features and Persian head-dresses and hairstyling.

- Bas-relief figures on stone slabs that once formed a giant frieze, show King Antiochus's ancestors standing before incense-burning altars.

- They also depict the king shaking hands with Apollo, Zeus, and Heracles—clearly, Antiochus wanted to show the world that he was on the best of terms with his gods.

▶ A MYSTERIOUS BREAKER'S YARD OF BROKEN STATUARY ON A COLOSSAL SCALE LITTERS THE REMOTE SUMMIT OF NEMRUT DAG IN TURKEY.

did you know?

...it's here?

Türkiye

Turkey

Nemrut Dag *Turkey*

When it is midday at Nemrut Dag it is 8pm at the Great Barrier Reef and 11am in Copenhagen…   …do you know where they are?

River Nile

> ➤ EGYPT'S GREAT RIVER IS THE LONGEST IN THE WORLD, COMBINING THE POWER OF THE BLUE NILE AND THE WHITE NILE AND FLOWING INTO THE MEDITERRANEAN SEA.

did **you** know?

...it's here?

origins &
controversy

- The Nile flows for 4,160 miles (6,695km) from its various sources into the fertile Nile Delta.

- It originates in the great lakes of Africa, with the two main branches—the Blue and White Niles—converging to the southeast of the city of Khartoum.

- The Blue Nile rises in Lake Tana, in the highlands of Ethiopia, slashing a gorge through the great Ethiopian plateau before flowing through the hot plains of southern Sudan.

- The White Nile flows comparably slowly from its source at Lake Victoria. Finding proof of the Nile's origin taxed many great European explorers in the mid-19th century, including John Speke, Richard Burton, David Livingstone, and Henry Morton Stanley.

- Control of the flow of water at the northern end of the Nile has been a contentious issue for many years, and now focuses on the Aswan High Dam, 600 miles (965km) from Cairo.

- The dam has allowed for year-round irrigation, and has given a major boost to local agriculture, but at the loss of valuable alluvial deposits further downstream.

- Sub-Saharan countries which suffer from severe droughts are keen to exploit the waters of the Nile too, and dispute its control by Egypt.

- When it is midday on the River Nile it is 3am at the Grand Canyon and 8pm in Vladivostok...   *...do you know where they are?*

Great Pyramid

construction & **burial**

- More than 2.25 million stone blocks were used in the construction of the pyramid, each weighing more than 2.75 tons.

- The Great Pyramid was built around 2589BC, and was first officially opened up in AD820.

- Wooden boats discovered buried in the sand beside the Great Pyramid were perhaps intended for the ruler's voyages in the afterlife.

pharaohs & **kings**

- The pyramid was probably built as the tomb of Pharaoh Kufu, also known as Cheops, but his body has never been found.

- Two later kings—Khafre and Menkaure—built their own pyramids close by, forming a unique group of pyramids, which are now Egypt's premier tourist attraction.

Q *What mysterious figure watches over the Great Pyramid?*

A *The Sphinx, built by Kufu's son, Khafre.*

▶ THE GREAT PYRAMID WHICH HAS STOOD AT THE EDGE OF THE DESERT, TO THE WEST OF THE RIVER NILE SINCE THE 26TH CENTURY BC, IS THE OUTSTANDING LEGACY OF THE ANCIENT EGYPTIANS.

did **you** know?

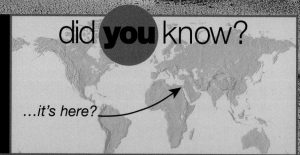

...it's here?

? Smaller pyramids nearby are believed to mark the location of the tombs of priests, officials and the wives of the pharaohs.

Q *How tall is the Great Pyramid?*

A 450 feet (137m).

~ When it is midday at the Great Pyramid, it is 11am at the Sagrada Família and 2am in Seattle...   ...do you know where they are?

Temple of Karnak

Egypt

معبد

▶ The largest temple complex in ancient Egypt, Karnak lay at the heart of the capital of Thebes, where the modern city of Luxor stands today.

did **you** know?

...it's here?

Temple of Karnak *Egypt*

Q In Egyptian mythology, what did the stone pillars of the temple represent?

A Palm trees from the island where all life began.

- At midday at the Temple of Karnak it is 3.30pm in the Himalayas and 5pm in Hanoi...   *...do you know where they are?*

TIME ZONE: TEMPLE OF KARNAK GMT+2

ancient &
venerated

- The settlement of Thebes, on the east bank of the River Nile and the capital of Egypt for some 1,500 years, has long since disappeared, and this temple is its only relic.

- With its imposing gates, courts, halls, forests of pillars, carvings, statues and obelisks, it was the biggest temple complex of its day.

- A number of different deities were worshiped here, and the principal one was Amun, god of the winds and the air. Amun was represented as a human figure with a double feather crown, and was worshiped as Egypt's national god in the 16th century BC, along with his consort, the goddess Mut, and son Khons, the moon god.

- Ten different areas of the Temple were accessed via huge portals, known as pylons. Each pylon was a vast doorway flanked by two massive towers.

- As the worshiper penetrated the temple, he passed from the sunlight of the outside world into the deepening darkness of successive halls, heading ever closer to the mystery of the inner shrine, which contained the image of the god.

- Processional avenues dramatically lined with sculptures of ram-headed sphinxes led up to the Temple of Karnak from the River Nile and from the city of Luxor itself.

Temple of Karnak *Egypt*

Jerusalem

holy &
embattled

- There are around 300 holy monuments and buildings in Jerusalem, which is divided into the New City and the walled Old City.

- Among the cobbled streets, markets, houses, and courtyards of the Old City are three of the city's most significant monuments: the superb Dome of the Rock, one of Islam's holiest shrines; the Wailing Wall, one of Judaism's most potent symbols; and the Church of the Holy Sepulchre, built over the spot where Jesus Christ was crucified.

- Jerusalem was founded by Canaanites around 3000BC. It was razed several times in its turbulent history, including in 586BC by Nebuchadnezzar, and in AD70 by the Romans.

- The city was partitioned between Jordan and Israel after the first Arab-Israeli War in 1948. However, in 1967, during the Six Day War, Israeli troops drove out the remaining Palestinians and seized control of the whole city.

Q *For whom do people traditionally pray at the Western ("Wailing") Wall?*

▶ JERUSALEM IS A CITY UNIQUELY SACRED TO THE JEWISH, CHRISTIAN, AND ISLAMIC FAITHS, AND REPRESENTS AROUND 5,000 YEARS OF HUMAN AND SPIRITUAL HISTORY.

did **you** know?

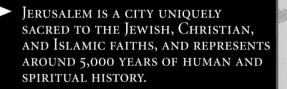

...it's here?

מדינת ישראל

A For the Jewish citizens killed or enslaved by the conquering Romans in AD70.

- At midday in Jerusalem it is 5am in Philadelphia and 11am on the Matterhorn... ...do you know where they are?

Dead Sea

concentrated &
saline

- The Dead Sea lies 1,300 feet (396m) below sea level, and has a concentration of mineral salts that is an extraordinary ten times higher than normal sea water.

- It's not even a sea, but rather a lake, fed by fresh water from the River Jordan and other small streams, and evaporated by the intense heat in this valley.

- The southern sector of the lake has hot springs and pools of mineral-rich black mud, both associated for centuries with healing and health-giving properties.

- Despite its extreme salinity—which makes bathers so buoyant it's easier to float than swim—the Dead Sea is not quite dead, but home to some salt-loving bacteria.

- It is made up of two basins that, together, stretch for a length of around 45 miles (72km), and a width of about 9 miles (14km).

▶ A VAST AND EXTRAORDINARY SALINE LAKE IN ISRAEL'S JORDAN VALLEY, THE DEAD SEA RENDERS TRADITIONAL SWIMMING SKILLS OBSOLETE.

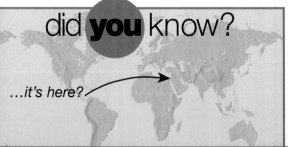

did **you** know?

...it's here?

Israel

מדינת ישראל

Q In the biblical tale, who was turned into a pillar of salt near the modern town of Sedom?

A Lot's wife.

At midday on the Dead Sea it is 10am in Marrakech and midnight at the Southern Alps... ...do you know where they are?

Petra

Q When were the secrets of Petra revealed to the world?

A In 1812, by Swiss explorer Johann Burckhardt.

▶ PETRA, THE LONG-LOST "ROSE-RED" CITY IN THE JORDANIAN DESERT, IS A MYSTERIOUS AND AWESOME MAN-MADE WONDER THAT CAN ONLY BE PARTLY EXPLAINED.

did **you** know?

...it's here?

secretive & **mysterious**

- Petra lies in the cleft of a dry river valley, or *wadi*, between Aqaba and the Dead Sea, on the eastern side of Wadi Arabah in Jordan, and is approached through a secret narrow pass called the Siq.

- Enormous facades have been cut straight into the faces of the rocks—which are salmon pink in reality, rather than the romantic "rose-red" as they were memorably described in a 19th-century poem.

- While the facades give the appearance of a grand, abandoned city created for giants—an image supported by names such as the Treasury—these are in fact the tombs which belonged to an ancient mud city that has long-since disappeared.

- They are the legacy of a nomadic tribe called the Nabataeans, who settled here in the sixth century BC at this favored location on a major trade route. Little is known of these people, but it seems that they made sacrifices to their gods (and possibly human sacrifices, at that).

- The massive and elegant stone facades of Petra show Nabataean crow-step decoration and superbly detailed classical styling, but it is disappointing to discover that the chambers behind these splendid frontages are completely bare and without ornament.

Great Palace

> ▶ ST. PETERSBURG'S GREAT PALACE, WITH ITS LAVISH FOUNTAINS AND MAGNIFICENT GARDENS, IS THE ULTIMATE SYMBOL OF RUSSIAN IMPERIAL GRANDEUR.

did **you** know?

...it's here?

РОССИЯ

gilded &
glorious

- Czar Peter the Great founded St. Petersburg in 1703, as a new capital for Russia that would reflect Western tastes and so draw his country into the modern world.

- St. Petersburg was built on rather unpromising swampland in the northeast of the country, overlooking the Gulf of Finland.

- Outside the new city, the czar planned for himself a palatial complex that would out-dazzle that most glittering of palaces, Versailles, complete with the latest fashion accessories: fountains and waterworks on a grand scale.

- The palace waterworks, which are spread over a 300-acre (121ha) park, require thousands of gallons of water to be pumped through every second. They include cascades and water spouts, some of which are designed to go off unexpectedly and drench unsuspecting passers-by.

- The palace itself, called Petrodvorets (Peter's Palace), was intended to be no less splendid than the waterworks, and later rulers made many additions and embellishments. It has been magnificently restored to its former glory in recent years.

At midday at the Great Palace it is 1am in Vancouver and 9am in the Sahara Desert…   *…do you know where they are?*

Kremlin

imposing &
impressive

- The Kremlin is triangular in shape, with one side bordering on the Moskva River, and covers almost 70 acres (28ha) of ground at the center of the city.

- Within its walls stand some of the city's most beautiful churches, as well as the 15th-century Granovitaya Palata with its throne room, the 19th-century Great Kremlin Palace where the Supreme Soviet government met, and the 20th-century building once used for Communist Party conferences.

▶ THE KREMLIN IS A VAST WALLED FORTRESS SITE IN THE MIDDLE OF THE RUSSIAN CAPITAL, MOSCOW, AN UNMISTAKABLE SEAT OF POWER AND AUTHORITY.

did **you** know?

...it's here?

РОССИЯ

? The Kremlin's brick walls were rebuilt in the late 15th century with 20 towers, some of which have distinctive tent-shaped steeples topped by illuminated red stars.

history &
treasures

● The citadel was the nucleus around which Moscow grew after its foundation in the 12th century. Ivan the Terrible was crowned Czar of All the Russias here in 1547.

● There are many different museums and treasure houses within the Kremlin today, displaying fine art, and items recalling the Russian royal family such as their bejeweled Fabergé eggs.

Q *Which great square stands just outside the Kremlin walls?*

A Red Square.

▶ *At midday in the Kremlin it is 1pm in Abu Dhabi and 5pm at the Potala Palace...*   *...do you know where they are?*

Rift Valley

East Africa

East Africa

▶ THE RIFT VALLEY OF EAST AFRICA
MARKS A SERIES OF SPLITS IN THE
EARTH'S CRUST THAT STRETCH FOR
THOUSANDS OF MILES.

did **you** know?

...it's here?

Q What do Samburu, Amboseli, and the Masai Mara have in common?

A They are all national reserves and parks in the Rift Valley.

At midday in the Rift Valley it is 3am in the Galapagos Islands and 4pm in Jakarta…   …do you know where they are?

Q Which 19th-century German geophysicist developed the theory of Continental Drift?

A Alfred Wegener (1880–1930).

Q Olduvai Gorge, near Ngorongoro, is famous for what?

A Hominid fossils, suggesting this is the birthplace of the human race.

geology &
wildlife

- The East African Rift Valley shows a massive split in the surface of the earth, and is one of the most notable geological features of the planet—to fly over it is like a living lesson in the theory of plate tectonics.

- The view from the top of the steep escarpment on one side is of a sweeping panorama across a deep, flat-bottomed valley, in places too wide to see the opposite escarpment.

- The Rift Valley has two main branches. The western arm reaches from Lake Malawi in the south, close to the Mozambique coast, then north along the line of the African lakes to the west of Lake Victoria. The eastern branch starts to the east of Lake Victoria, then heads north through Tanzania and Kenya and into Ethiopia.

- Earthquakes and volcanic activity, both signs of an active rift in the earth's crust, are mostly confined to the northern area around the Afar Triangle.

- Lengai, in Tanzania, is the only active carbonatite volcano in the world—the lava is like a volcanic limestone that turns the color of dirty snow within a day of erupting.

- The East African Rift Valley is famous for its wildlife, and the Ngorongoro Crater is the location of Africa's finest game reserve, where elephants and lions are among the inhabitants.

The Himalayas

 Mount Everest, also known by its Nepalese name Chomolungma, is 29,028 feet (8,848m) high.

▶ THE GREATEST MOUNTAIN RANGE ON EARTH, THE HIMALAYAS ARE TOPPED BY MOUNT EVEREST, THE HIGHEST PEAK IN THE WORLD.

did **you** know?

...they're here?

Nepal Adhirajya

dramatic &
extensive

- The Himalayan mountain range includes the Karakoram Mountains, and stretches for more than 1,500 miles (2,415km), effectively dividing the Indian subcontinent to the south from Asia in the north.

- Territorially, the Himalayas lie partly in Nepal, partly with India, Sikkim, and Bhutan, and partly inside the boundaries of China (Tibet).

- The mountains have been created at a point where several land masses collide, buckling and pushing the earth's surface upwards, and forming jagged stone peaks.

- Ninety-six Himalayan peaks stand higher than 24,000 feet (7,315m)—and there are only 13 mountains of a similar scale to be found in the rest of the world.

- Many European mountaineers set out to climb and conquer Everest from the 19th century onwards, but it was a New Zealander, Edmund Hillary, who made the first successful ascent, accompanied by the Nepalese sherpa Tenzing Norgay, in 1953. The expedition took seven weeks all together.

- In 2004 the 26-year-old Nepalese sherpa, Pemba Darji, set a remarkable new world record by climbing to the summit in just over eight hours.

– At midday in the Himalayas it is 3.30am in Rio de Janeiro and 6.30am at Edinburgh Castle...   ...do you know where they are?

Taj Mahal

honor & architecture

- The Taj Mahal was built by Shah Jehan, the Moghul Emperor of India, as a tomb worthy of his beloved queen Mumtaz Mahal, and the building takes its name from an abbreviation of her name.

- Mumtaz Mahal was a shrewd political advisor as well as a much-loved wife, and died in 1631 at the age of just 36 while giving birth to the couple's 14th child.

- The building has a central pearl-shaped dome with four smaller domes, and four towers. The symmetry of this extraordinarily beautiful structure is reflected in the long pools of the formal gardens that surround it.

- The stonework reflects or soaks up the ever-changing light, looking pearly, pink, gold, or dazzling white. The marble surfaces are inlaid with intricate patterns of precious and semi-precious stones, and calligraphic decoration of inlaid black marble, an outstanding example of craftsmanship that is still practised in the nearby town today.

robbery & restoration

- The silver doors of the tomb, a gold railing, and a cloth of pearls that lay over the queen's cenotaph, directly above the burial place, were stolen by thieves many years ago.

- The door of the entrance gateway was also of solid silver, and studded with hundreds of silver nails—and is also long gone.

- Inlaid jewels have also been prised from the walls, but despite this the magnificence still remains overwhelming.

- A much worse theft was nearly committed in the 1830s, when the building had become neglected and overgrown: William Bentinck, the Governor General of Bengal, proposed dismantling the Taj Mahal and selling off the marble in London. Fortunately this destructive money-making scheme was abandoned when it was realized that potential buyers were simply not very interested.

- Lord Curzon, Viceroy of India from 1900, restored the building to its former glory.

▶ THE TAJ MAHAL AT AGRA IN UTTAR PRADESH IN THE NORTH OF INDIA, IS THE SUBLIME MEMORIAL TO SHAH JEHAN'S WIFE, AND THE PINNACLE OF MOGHUL ARCHITECTURE.

did **you** know?

...it's here?

Bhārat Gaṇarājya

► *At midday at the Taj Mahal it is 12.30pm in Novosibirsk and 8.30pm at Nemrut Dag...*   *...do you know where they are?*

Red Fort

palace &
museum

- The Red Fort in Delhi was constructed for Shah Jehan between 1638 and 1648, when he moved his capital here from Agra.

- The walled complex originally included six royal palaces, and survivors of these include the Rang Mahal, or painted palace (though its paintings and silver ceilings are long gone), and the Mumtaz Mahal, now a museum.

- The grand buildings and audience chambers were once lined with opulent marble, silver, gold, and jewels, and while these were plundered long ago, the red sandstone structure still provides a vast and majestic glimpse of an imperial past.

- Marble panels removed from the Red Fort by the British after the Indian uprising of 1857 were restored to their rightful position in the early 20th century by Lord Curzon.

- Other buildings here include the Diwan-i-khas, a chamber specially for private consultations between the emperor and foreign ambassadors.

▶ THIS VAST IMPERIAL PALACE COMPLEX OF BRIGHT RED SANDSTONE AT DELHI IS THE OTHER GREAT LEGACY OF THE MOGHUL EMPEROR, SHAH JEHAN.

did **you** know?

...it's here?

Q *What is the name of the main entrance to the Red Fort?*

A *The Lahore Gate.*

Wat Phra Kaew

▶ Bangkok's Temple of the Emerald Buddha is Thailand's most sacred temple. It contains the country's most revered and sacred image.

did **you** know?

...it's here?

icons &
images

- The Emerald Buddha statue, carved from jade, stands just 31 inches (79cm) tall, and has had an eventful life.

- Its origin is unknown, but the figure is first recorded in 1434, when it was coated in stucco plaster—which later crumbled away.

- King Tilok of Lannathai acquired the statue and enshrined it in his capital, Chiang Mai. When the capital moved to Viang Chan, so did the Emerald Buddha, and when King Rama I built *his* new capital at Bangkok, he immediately constructed a splendid new temple to hold the image.

- Three more important statues of Buddha stand before the high altar in the Wat Phra Kaew. They were dedicated by the kings Rama III and Rama IV to their royal predecessors.

- Murals above the windows in the temple depict the life of Buddha, from his birth and childhood, through his renunciation of wealth and material gain in favor of the search for Truth, to his temptation and enlightenment, and eventual death.

historic &
dazzling

- The Wat Phra Kaew is just one of more than 100 buildings within the walls of Bangkok's Grand Palace, which covers an area of 2.3 million square feet (214,000 sq m).

- Built to house the revered Emerald Buddha, this superbly decorated temple was completed and consecrated in 1784.

- From the outside, the temple dazzles all the senses, from its gilded walls and carved figures to the tinkling bells along the roofline. Inside, it is no less ornamented.

Ayutthaya

structure &
significance

- Palaces, pagodas, and the remains of more than 400 Buddhist monasteries hint at the scale and importance of this city before its destruction by the Burmese in 1767.

- Many structures were restored or rebuilt during the 20th century, including the Tri Muk building—a wooden structure with brick foundations—and three *chedis*, or bell towers, dating back to the 15th century.

- At the heart of Ayutthaya was the Ancient Palace, built by the city's 14th-century founder, King U-Thong, and extended during the reigns of his various successors.

- Two temples, the Wat Phra Mahathat and the nearby Wat Tatburana, both revealed hidden treasures when they were restored in the 1950s, including a relic of Buddha in a golden casket, and royal regalia.

- Today there is a research institute on the site, including a museum, and showing detailed models of the reconstructed city.

> A SIAMESE CAPITAL FOR MORE THAN 400 YEARS, AND LOCATED JUST A DAY AWAY FROM MODERN BANGKOK, AYUTTHAYA IS A RUINED CITY THAT EVOKES A GLORIOUS PAST.

did **you** know?

...it's here?

Ayutthaya *Thailand*

Q What is the modern name of the ancient kingdom of Siam?

A Thailand.

At midday in Ayutthaya it is midnight at Niagara Falls and 6am in Stockholm...   ...do you know where they are?

Potala Palace

► THE IMPERIOUS POTALA PALACE AT LHASA WAS BUILT AS THE HOME OF THE DALAI LAMA, THE SPIRITUAL LEADER OF TIBETAN BUDDHISTS.

did **you** know?

...it's here?

中华人民共和国

important &
historic

- The palace stands on a high outcrop of rock called Marpori (the Red Hill), looming about 300 feet (91m) above the holy city of Lhasa, and derives its name from a Sanskrit word meaning "Buddha's mountain."

- It was built between 1645 and 1694 on the orders of the fifth Dalai Lama, the ruler of Tibet.

- The Potala Palace was the winter residence of the Dalai Lamas until 1959, when the 14th Dalai Lama fled to the sanctuary of India, following an unsuccessful uprising against the Chinese occupation of the country (an occupation which continues, controversially, to this day).

- Today the 14th Dalai Lama continues to live in Dharamsala, in India, as the exiled head of state and spiritual leader of the Tibetan people. Born into a peasant family from northeast Tibet in 1935, he was identified as the new incarnation of the Dalai Lama at the age of just two. In 1989 he was awarded the Nobel Peace Prize for his continuing efforts to find a peaceful solution to his country's troubles.

vast &
multi-purpose

- The palace is huge and has more than 1,000 rooms, where the treasures including a staggering 10,000 shrines and 20,000 statues.

- The palace once contained libraries, government offices, a monastic training school, meditation halls, armories, and even a dungeon. There is now a museum inside the palace.

- At midday at the Potala Palace it is 5am at the Colosseum and 7am in Kuwait...   *...do you know where they are?*

Forbidden City

insular &
protected

- The Forbidden City was built by Emperor Yongle in the 15th century, inside the Imperial City—which was also square and had its own defensive walls.

- It was the home of the rulers of the Ming and Qing dynasties for nearly 500 years, until the fall of the empire in 1911.

- It reached the height of its glory in the 18th century, with the building of new temples, palaces, and gateways, and the construction of beautiful lakes and gardens.

- The emperor lived in the Forbidden City with his wives and concubines, and a veritable army of eunuchs and servants. Life was governed by a strict and elaborate code of rules, formal etiquette, and taboos.

- The biggest building here is the Hall of Supreme Harmony, entered via a massive red-laquered gateway—it is where the emperors would sit enthroned for grand state occasions.

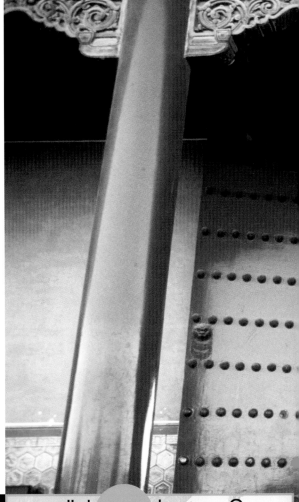

▶ CUT OFF BY ITS MOAT AND HIGH PURPLE WALL, CLOSED TO ORDINARY MORTALS, THE FORBIDDEN CITY WAS A CITY WITHIN A CITY AT THE HEART OF BEIJING.

did **you** know?

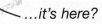

...it's here?

中华人民共和国

Forbidden City *China*

Q In which direction do all the major buildings in the Forbidden City face?

A South, turning away from Siberian winds and hostile supernatural forces.

- At midday in the Forbidden City it is 4pm in Suva and 8pm at Yosemite National Park...   ...do you know where they are?

Great Wall of China

power &
glory

- The wall dates from 220BC. It was built by the ruthless and savage despot, Qin Shihuangdi, who became the first man to rule a united China. The wall stands 30 feet (9m) high on average.

- The wall served a dual purpose: to keep out the Mongolian horsemen who threatened from the plains to the north; and as a clear assertion of one man's power.

- Qin Shihuangdi was a keen builder, and went on to use forced labor to construct roads and canals as well. He standardized Chinese script and coinage as well as weights and measures.

completion &
repair

- Nicknamed the Wall of Tears, the Great Wall was built by a conscripted army of peasants, soldiers, convicts, and political prisoners, and it is said that the bodies of the thousands who died were used to fill and cement it.

- The new wall linked some existing sections, but the sheer scale of the build is difficult to comprehend: the wall extends for around 4,000 miles (6,437km), from Bo Hai Sea northeast of Beijing, across China and into the Gobi Desert.

- The wall has been restored and rebuilt many times over, and remains one of the most remarkable engineering feats of all time.

> ► CHINA'S EXTRAORDINARY GREAT WALL WAS BUILT AS A STATEMENT OF IMPERIAL POWER IN JUST TEN YEARS, AT THE HUMAN COST OF THOUSANDS OF LIVES.

did **you** know?

...it's here?

China

中华人民共和国

Great Wall of China *China*

103

- At midday at the Great Wall of China it is 5am at Versailles and 2pm at the Great Barrier Reef... ...do you know where they are?

Borobudur

 The name Borobudur means simply "many Buddhas."

➤ FOR THE INHABITANTS OF THE INDONESIAN ISLAND OF JAVA, ANCIENT BOROBUDUR WAS THE GIANT MYTHOLOGICAL PEAK ON WHICH THE UNIVERSE RESTS.

did **you** know?

...it's here?

Republik Indonesia

stone-built &
terraced

- This extraordinary monument, dating to around AD800, is a stepped pyramid of receding terraces built over the top of a hill, and is said to be the largest Buddhist shrine in the world.

- It is built entirely of stone, which is highly carved, and at its highest point it stands 1,310 feet (400m) high. It was built by an enormous workforce under the control of the Saliendra dynasty of rulers, probably over the course of several decades.

- Five lower, square-shaped terraces represent the material world, while the three circular terraces above them represent the spiritual realm, closer to the sky.

- On the upper terraces there are distinctive rows of stupas—that is, large shrines of stone pierced and carved to look like giant upturned handbells. Each stupa contains a statue of Buddha.

- A single shrine at the top, in the middle of the highest terrace and with a fabulous view over the surrounding mountains, represents nirvana—that is, spiritual freedom, or heaven.

- Borobudur is Java's distinctive representation of Mount Meru, a giant golden peak which is described in Indian mythology as the point upon which the entire universe rests.

art &
craftsmanship

- The monument is most famous for its carved stone panels. There are around 1,500 of these, and they depict scenes from the life of Buddha. Hundreds more carvings show the everyday life of ordinary citizens.

- The site was abandoned after just 200 years, and only rediscovered in the 19th century by an English army officer.

Itsukushima Shrine

sacred &
poignant

- Miyajima Island is so sacred that for many centuries it was forbidden for anyone either to be born or to die there. Elderly people, people who were sick, and women who became pregnant were all taken away to the mainland. The deer on the island are protected and dogs are also banned from here.

- The shrine is set on wooden piles in a small bay on Japan's southern coastline, and at high tide the various buildings, linked by covered walkways, appear to float on the sea.

- The shrine is principally dedicated to three Shinto goddesses—the daughters of the storm god Susano, who is a major Japanese deity. There are also shrines on the site to one of Susano's sons, Okinonushi.

- The shrine's best-known feature is its magnificent red-painted wooden *torii*, or portal, which stands alone in the water, 53 feet (16m) high, and with a curved lintel 76 feet (23m) long.

▶ THIS BEAUTIFUL SHINTO SHRINE IS SITUATED IN A BAY OF THE SACRED MIYAJIMA ISLAND, NOT FAR FROM THE REBUILT JAPANESE CITY OF HIROSHIMA.

did **you** know?

...it's here?

日本国

Q In what year was nearby Hiroshima devastated by the first ever atom bomb?

A In 1945.

Itsukushima Shrine *Japan*

> At midday at the Itsukushima Shrine it is 5am in Johannesburg and 7pm at the Hoover Dam...   ...do you know where they are?

Uluru

location &
scale

- Uluru lies near the township of Alice Springs in the desert heart of the Australian continent, and forms the largest exposed monolith in the world.

- It is 1.5 miles (2.4km) long, 1 mile (1.6km) wide and towers 1,143 feet (348m) above the dry plain, catching the light of the rising and setting sun and appearing to change color dramatically.

> ▶ AUSTRALIA'S MOST FAMOUS NATURAL WONDER IS THE MASSIVE MONOLITH OF RED SANDSTONE, WHICH IS IN THE NORTHERN TERRITORY IN THE HEART OF THE COUNTRY.

did **you** know?

...it's here?

TIME ZONE: ULURU GMT+9.5

Australia

culture &
palette

- Uluru has been important to the Local Aboriginal people, Anangu, for centuries, and they are now its official custodians.

- Anangu paintings may be seen around the base of the rock, and the people regard it as disrespectful to climb on the rock, although this activity is not prohibited.

- The distinctive red color of Uluru is down to the weathering of the rock, an arkose sandstone with a high iron content and a rich blend of feldspar minerals.

Q *In which of Australia's national parks will you find Uluru?*

A *Uluru-Kata Tjuta National Park.*

At midday at Uluru it is 2.30am at the Leaning Tower of Pisa and 12.30pm in Brisbane...   *...do you know where they are?*

Sydney Opera House

Q How much did it cost to build?

A More than $AU100 million.

▶ ON SYDNEY'S SHELTERED HARBOR STANDS A FABULOUS STRUCTURE OF PEAKED WHITE ROOFS, RECOGNIZED INSTANTLY THE WORLD OVER.

did **you** know?

...it's here?

Sydney Opera House *Australia*

Swedish &
Danish connections

- In 1957 the competition to design the new opera house attracted 222 entries from 32 different countries.

- The 'sails' of the opera house roof are covered with more than 1 million ceramic tiles, which were made in Sweden.

- The opera hall seats 1,500 people and the concert hall seats 2,700 people.

- The Opera House was designed by Danish architect Jørn Utzon, who was inspired by the yacht sails in Sydney harbor.

- When Utzon resigned just three years into the project, the role of engineers Ove Arup became critical to its completion.

- The Opera House was opened in October 1973 by Queen Elizabeth II.

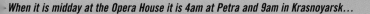

When it is midday at the Opera House it is 4am at Petra and 9am in Krasnoyarsk...   *...do you know where they are?*

Great Barrier Reef

protected &
alive

- The Great Barrier Reef is protected as a World Heritage Site, a Biosphere Reserve, and a national marine park—in biological, geological, and scientific terms, it is recognized as one of the greatest natural wonders of the world.

- The reef extends for around 1,250 miles (2,012km) from Lady Elliot Island to the tip of Cape York—shallow coastal waters which support a huge diversity of marine species.

- It is believed that the first corals started to inhabit this area around 17 million years ago.

- The reef itself is made up of tiny, primitive living animals or coral polyps, which live in a thin veneer over the bulky build-up of the empty skeletons of past generations—the coral itself is a soft body surrounded by an exoskeleton of limestone.

- The coral thrives in unpolluted waters that maintain a constant temperature of between 72°F and 82°F (22°C and 28°C).

▶ THIS WONDER OF THE MARINE WORLD LIES OFF THE EASTERN SEABOARD OF AUSTRALIA, A FRAGILE ECOSYSTEM UNDER THREAT FROM NATURAL OR HUMAN DISASTER.

did **you** know?

...it's here?

diversity &
wildlife

- There are more than 400 species of coral on the Great Barrier Reef, and they take on forms described by terms such as staghorn and brain.

- The reef also supports more than 1,500 species of fish, six of the seven species of sea turtle in the world, and more than 240 species of waders and seabirds, including sea eagles.

Great Barrier Reef *Australia*

At midday at the Great Barrier Reef it is 3am in Carthage and 10am at the Potala Palace...   ...do you know where they are?

Rotorua

Q *When was Rotorua's landmark mock-Tudor Bath House built?*

A *In 1908.*

▶ THE BEST-KNOWN GEOTHERMAL
CENTER IN THE SOUTHERN
HEMISPHERE IS TO BE FOUND ON
NEW ZEALAND'S NORTH ISLAND,
AROUND THE TOWN OF ROTORUA.

did **you** know?

...it's here?

New Zealand

sulphurous &
natural

- Natural hot springs and pools for bathing, sulphurous mud for healing, and colorful, steaming lakes are the main elements that have brought generations of tourists to this geothermal wonderland.

- Nowhere in the town is far from thermal activity of one sort or another, from the plumes of steam that punctuate the green spaces of the public parks, to the hotel spas, and Hinemoa's hot pool on Mokoia Island.

- North Island also has a chain of sleeping volcanoes in the Tongariro National Park, directly south of here along the same geological fault line. Mount Ruapehu was the last to have a serious eruption in 1995 and 1996.

extreme &
colorful

- On the edge of Rotorua, the Whakarewarewa thermal reserve is the place to see the extraordinary hissing plume of the Pohutu geyser, which vents up to 100 feet (30m) high at intervals of 20 minutes.

- Waimangu, southeast of the town, is famous for its blue and green lakes of hot water stained with minerals. It lies in the crater of an extinct volcano.

- Wai-O-Tapu, also to the south, has the Artist's Palette (a steaming silica field in pale yellow, green, and blue) and the Champagne Pool (which, at 165°F/74°C is anything but chilled).

· At midday at Rotorua it is 6pm at Teotihuacán and midnight in Casablanca...   *...do you know where they are?*

Southern Alps

New Zealand

New Zealand

> ➤ THE GLACIERS OF NEW ZEALAND'S SOUTHERN ALPS ARE REMARKABLE FOR THEIR BEAUTY, ACCESSIBILITY, AND FOR THEIR DESCENT INTO SUBTROPICAL RAINFOREST.

did **you** know?

…they are here?

TIME ZONE: SOUTHERN ALPS GMT+12

➤ At midday at the Southern Alps it is 7pm at Niagara Falls and 2am in Istanbul…   …do you know where they are?

mountains &
snowfall

- The Southern Alps form a high mountain barrier down the western side of New Zealand's South Island, and from the highest point, Mount Cook (12,349 feet/3,764m), it is only 20 miles (32km) to the Pacific coastline.

- Westerly winds that blow in from the Tasman Sea are laden with moisture. This moisture falls as snow on the tops of the mountains, steadily feeding and renewing the glaciers that pour down the mountains.

- The most famous of these glaciers are the Fox and Franz Josef glaciers to the west, and the Tasman to the east.

- The Fox and Franz Josef glaciers are both relatively short and steep, tumbling down into subtropical, evergreen rainforest in an extraordinary juxtaposition.

? A tension crack in the surface of a glacier, formed as the ice grinds sowly downhill, is called a crevass.

longest &
broadest

- The Tasman Glacier is the largest in New Zealand. It is up to 2,000 feet (610m) thick in places and is 17 miles (27km) long.

- It is named after the Dutch navigator Abel Tasman (1603–c.1659), the first European explorer to set foot in the country (although he didn't stay long).

- Originating on the flanks of Mount Cook, it broadens to as wide as 2 miles (3km) and flows at a rate of 20–25 inches (51–64cm) per day, reaching almost as far as the South Island's central plain.

- The Tasman Glacier is gradually retreating, as its snout melts more quickly than the speed of its flow. This is due to its relatively low height above sea level where the temperatures are comparatively warm.

Hawaiian Islands

Q *Kauai is one of the loveliest of the Hawaiian islands. What is its other claim to fame?*

A *It is one of the wettest places on earth, averaging 460 inches (1,170cm) of rain each year.*

▶ THE ISLANDS OF HAWAII FORM A LUSH, VOLCANIC ARCHIPELAGO IN THE PACIFIC OCEAN, PERCHED ABOVE A "HOT SPOT" IN THE EARTH'S CRUST.

did **you** know?

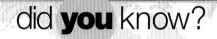

...they're here?

TIME ZONE: HAWAIIAN ISLANDS GMT-10

Hawaiian Islands *USA*

volcanic &
volatile

- All the islands in the Hawaiian chain are volcanic, with the oldest located at the western end and the youngest (and therefore the most active) at the eastern end, culminating in Hawaii island itself.

- The islands stretch for about 1,500 miles (2,415km) across the Pacific Ocean. Despite their volcanic origins, they are not directly part of the so-called Ring of Fire—the volcanoes that lie around the margin of the Pacific Ocean.

- Most of the current volcanic activity on Hawaii is on Kilauea, a subsidiary volcano which sits on the side of Hawaii's second highest mountain, Mauna Loa. Kilauea erupted almost continuously during the 19th century, and has been active again since 1983.

- Kilauea's crater is around 160 feet (49m) deep, and covers an area of 4 square miles (10.4 sq km).

- According to local lore, Kilauea is the home of Pele, the goddess of volcanoes, and the low-pitched humming or roaring which precedes some eruptions here is said to be evidence of her voice.

? The height and clear, unpolluted atmosphere of Mauna Kea, Hawaii's highest mountain, have made it perfect as the site for powerful astronomical telescopes.

- At midday on the Hawaiian Islands it is midnight in Helsinki and 4am at the Kapellbrücke...   ...do you know where they are?

Redwoods & Giant Sequoias

Q *What's the estimated weight of the largest giant sequoia, known as General Sherman?*

A *4.4 million pounds (2 million kg).*

high & mighty

- Both redwoods and giant sequoias live for a very long time—up to 3,000 years for the redwoods, and 4,000 years for the giant sequoias. Both species of tree have been around since the Jurassic period (about 200 million years).

- Both species grow straight with few knots, and produce very high quality timber that is suitable for a wide range of uses, including building houses, making furniture, and even the manufacture of railway sleepers.

- A combination of natural oils and resins in the timber makes it highly resistant to rot and termites, and exploitation of these valuable trees in the 19th century brought both species close to extinction.

- Today they are protected in the Redwood National Park of North California, and in the Sequoia National Park in the center of the same state.

> THESE TRUE GIANTS OF THE FORESTS GROW ALONG THE WESTERN COAST OF NORTH AMERICA, AND INLAND ON THE SLOPES OF THE SIERRA NEVADA MOUNTAINS.

did **you** know?

...they are here?

123

➤ *At midday among the redwoods and giant sequoias it is 10am at the Metéora monasteries…*　　　*…do you know where they are?*

Golden Gate Bridge

▶ SINCE ITS OPENING IN 1937, THE GOLDEN GATE BRIDGE HAS PROVIDED THE LINK ACROSS THE BAY BETWEEN THE CITY OF SAN FRANCISCO AND MARIN COUNTY.

did **you** know?

◀ ...it's here?

Golden Gate Bridge *USA*

Q How many cars cross the bridge daily?

A Around 125,000, not to mention the pedestrians.

towers &
high tides

● The towers rise 746ft (227m) above the level of high tide, to allow shipping to pass beneath.

● Each suspension cable is 36.5in (93cm) in diameter, and composed of more than 27,000 separate strands of wire.

● A vast 1,000-acre (405-ha) park lies to the south of the bridge, stretching almost half way across San Francisco.

Q What was the most dangerous part of the construction process?

A Laying the foundations for the south tower, while dealing with huge tidal swells.

When it is midday at the Golden Gate Bridge it is 4pm at the Inca Trails and 9pm in Geneva...   ...do you know where they are?

125

Yosemite National Park

valley & **park**

- The valley lies in the heart of the Sierra Nevada mountains of California, and extends for 7.5 miles (12km).

- Yosemite National Park takes in a total area of 1,189 square miles (3,080sq km). Within the boundaries of the park are the Merced River, Yosemite Falls, Mariposa Grove (a cluster of giant sequoias which are thousands of years old), and some high rocky peaks.

Q *Which Scottish naturalist influenced the national parks strategy in the USA?*

A *John Muir (1838–1914).*

▶ THE YOSEMITE VALLEY BECAME THE FIRST EVER STATE PARK IN THE USA IN 1864, AND ITS BEAUTY AND DIVERSITY HAVE BEEN PROTECTED EVER SINCE.

did **you** know?

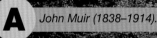

...it's here?

heights &
highlights

- Tuolumne Meadows is an area of high country where huge rock domes tower over lush, green meadows and crystal-clear lakes.

- El Capitan, an almost sheer granite buttress, 3,605 feet (1,099m) from the valley floor, is the highlight for rock-climbers.

Yosemite National Park *USA*

127

- At midday at Yosemite National Park it is 3pm at the Lincoln Memorial and 9pm in Dubrovnik...   *...do you know where they are?*

Hoover Dam

► THIS MASSIVE DAM IN THE MIDDLE OF THE DESERT, TAMES THE COLORADO RIVER. IT WAS BEGUN IN 1931 AND WAS NAMED AFTER THE PRESIDENT OF THE DAY, HERBERT CLARK HOOVER.

did **you** know?

...it's here?

concrete &
clay

- It was decided that a dam was needed after the Colorado River unexpectedly changed course in 1905, threatening to flood the Imperial Valley. It would also improve irrigation in the area, and generate electricity.

- When word got out that the dam building project was to go ahead, unemployed men flocked to the desert from all parts of the USA, hoping for laboring jobs. The initial camps and shanty towns eventually made way for the growth of Boulder City, built partly to keep the workers away from the distractions of Las Vegas.

- More than 7 million tons of rock had to be excavated before construction work could even begin on the dam.

- The dam contains as much steel in its structure as New York's Empire State Building, and stands 726 feet (221m) high—that's about the same height as a 70-story skyscraper.

- Immediately to the north, the dam created Lake Mead, one of the largest manmade reservoirs in the world. Today it is run by the National Park Service as a leisure facility and is used for sailing and other watersports.

Q *What name did President Roosevelt give the dam when he formally dedicated it in 1936?*

A *The Boulder Dam—it reverted to the name Hoover Dam in 1947.*

- At midday at the Hoover Dam it is 6am at Sydney Opera House and 10pm in Cape Town...   *...do you know where they are?*

Grand Canyon

deep &
wide

- The canyon is a massive gorge up to 18 miles (29km) wide, cut by the Colorado River. The river is now reduced to what looks like a brown trickle in the bottom, but is still, in fact, a powerful force when you see it up close.

- Movements in the earth's surface around 10 million years ago caused the land to rise, and the river started to cut a channel through the rock, eroding first the softer limestones, then the older shales and sandstones.

- The hardest and oldest rocks, 2 billion-year-old schists and granites, were less susceptible to erosion by water, and today they form the bottom of the canyon.

- The colored strata of the cliffs, seen along the gorge and its many branches, are one of its most remarkable features. Light and shadow cause constant color changes from black and purple-brown to pale pink, blue-gray, and every shade of orange and ocher.

► THE SHEER SIZE OF THE GRAND CANYON IN NORTHWEST ARIZONA MAKES IT A BREATHTAKING SIGHT, HOWEVER MANY TIMES IN YOUR LIFE YOU SEE IT.

did **you** know?

...it's here?

Grand Canyon *USA*

- At midday at the Grand Canyon it is 2pm in Bogotá and 9pm at the Temple of Karnak…   *…do you know where they are?*

Zion National Park

► KNOWN FOR ITS REMARKABLE ROCK FORMATIONS, UTAH'S ZION NATIONAL PARK WAS DESIGNATED FOR PROTECTION AS EARLY AS 1919.

did **you** know?

...it's here?

USA

dramatic &
biblical

- The focus of the park is Zion Canyon, a river-cut gorge like a smaller version of the Grand Canyon, reaching a depth of 2,500 feet (762m) and dramatic in its own right.

- The gorge is cut through Navajo pinkish-red sandstone, revealing the older Kaibab limestone underneath.

- The park is famous for its weird and wonderful rock formations, such as the Checkerboard Mesa—a sandstone outcrop looming over a road, its surface neatly carved into squares by the effects of wind and water.

- Zion was discovered and named by Mormons in the 1860s, and the highest point in the park is known as the West Temple. The biblical references continue with formations called the Towers of the Virgin and the Temple of Sinawava.

Zion National Park *USA*

▶ At midday at Zion National Park it is 8pm in Warsaw and 9pm at the Parthenon...   ...do you know where they are?

Teotihuacán

sophisticated & **extensive**

- Teotihuacán was founded around AD450, and grew to be the largest city in Mesoamerica. Its name means "place of the gods."

- The city had everything, from town planning on a strict grid, to wide streets, monumental religious buildings, artisans' quarters, and private dwellings.

- Little is known of the daily life of the people who lived here, other than they worshiped a rain god and revered the jaguar.

- Stone carvings here would have made an even greater impression in their day, when they were decorated with stucco, obsidian (a glassy volcanic rock), and paintwork.

- The city was destroyed and burned around AD700, but today its stone ruins still reveal richly carved and decorated temples, three pyramids associated with worship, as well as two public gathering places—the Citadel and the Great Compound.

▶ A SOPHISTICATED AND SPLENDID AZTEC CITY WITH PYRAMIDS AND TEMPLES ONCE FLOURISHED 20 MILES (32KM) NORTHEAST OF MEXICO CITY.

did **you** know?

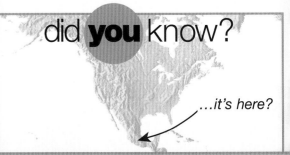

...it's here?

México

Teotihuacán *Mexico*

Q Which carved god is this, guarding a temple of the same name?

A Quetzalcoatl, the plumed serpent.

135

➤ At midday at Teotihuacán it is 2am in Shanghai and 8pm at Pamukkale... ...do you know where they are?

Chichén Itzá

> ▶ BUILT AS THE MAYAN CAPITAL ON THE YUCATAN PENINSULA AROUND AD1000, CHICHÉN ITZÁ WAS LATER TAKEN OVER BY THE TOLTECS AND INCREASED IN IMPORTANCE.

did **you** know?

...it's here?

México

built &
abandoned

- The city was built as a new capital dedicated to the ruler-god Kukulcan (also known by his Toltec name, Topltzin Quetzalcoatl), with a major pyramid-shaped temple called El Castillo (the castle) in his honor.

- As the Mayan civilization went into decline, Toltec warriors seized control and changed and extended the city, probably along the same lines as their own lost capital of Tula.

- The entire settlement is believed to have been abandoned around 1224, following an attack by a rival power. From this time onwards, the whole Toltec civilization across Mexico went into decline.

sites &
remains

- The extensive remains are an intriguing fusion of the ideas and motifs of both the Mayan and Toltec cultures.

- El Castillo is set exactly so that its four stepped sides face north, south, east, and west, with the carved serpent god's tail at the foot and its head at the top of the main staircase.

- Another unusual feature is the wonderfully preserved ball court, measuring 272 feet (83m) by 27 feet (8m). The precise game played here is unclear, but bas-relief carvings suggest that the loser also lost his head!

► At midday at Chichén Itzá it is 3pm at Iguassu Falls and 7pm in Monte Carlo...   ...do you know where they are?

137

Galapagos Islands

flora & **wildlife**

- These islands—with 15 main islands, 42 smaller ones and a further 26 rocks or reefs—are volcanic in origin, and stretch for 186 miles (300km) from north to south.

- The habitat is arid and dry along the coastal fringes, with lush, evergreen forest growing in the humidity of the hills, and open areas on the tops where sedges and ferns grow.

- Many of the animal species and subspecies found on the islands are unique not only to the Galapagos, but also to specific islands within the group. Wildlife includes two types of seal, seven kinds of marine iguana, bats, and rats—including a recently discovered race of giant rats.

- Galapagos finches, which have adapted to different niche habitats across the islands, are perhaps the most famous birds here. The islands are also the home of the largest colony of masked boobies in the world, as well as an indigenous species of penguin.

? The English naturalist Charles Darwin visited the islands in 1835, and many things he saw here inspired his great thesis, *The Origin of Species*.

▶ THE GALAPAGOS ISLANDS, A REMOTE ARCHIPELAGO IN THE PACIFIC OCEAN, ARE FAMOUS FOR THE RICH VARIETY OF THEIR UNIQUE FLORA AND FAUNA.

did **you** know?

...they're here?

República del Ecuador

Ecuador

Q What was the name of Darwin's ship?   **A** HMS Beagle.

➤ *At midday on the Galapagos Islands it is 6pm in Fez Medina and 11pm in Islamabad…*   *…do you know where they are?*

Machu Picchu

▶ HIGH IN THE MOUNTAINS OF THE PERUVIAN ANDES LIE THE REMAINS OF A MYSTERIOUS SETTLEMENT, ITS ORIGINS AND EXACT PURPOSE OBSCURE AND UNKNOWN.

did **you** know?

...it's here?

TIME ZONE: MACHU PICCHU GMT-5

República del Perú

obscurity &
rediscovery

- So little is known about the site that even its name is lost in obscurity—in modern times, following its rediscovery in the early 20th century, it was given the name Machu Picchu, after a local mountain peak.

- It is an Inca site, probably dating from the expansion of the Inca empire at the end of the 15th century, and has around 200 buildings including residences, storehouses, and temples.

- The population may have numbered only about 1,500 people, and analysis of skeletons found here shows that women outnumbered men by 10 to 1, suggesting that this might have been a sanctuary for women known as the Virgins of the Sun.

- Theories of sun worship are bolstered by the existence of the Intihuatana, or Hitching Post of the Sun, a complicated astronomical device, and by temples and observatories linked to the winter and summer solstices.

- Machu Picchu has survived because it was so well built—the craftsmanship of its stonework terraces and structures, which were built entirely without the use of mortar, is remarkable.

Q Who rediscovered Machu Picchu in 1911?

A Yale archaeologist and politician, Hiram Bingham (1875–1956).

At midday at Machu Picchu it is 9am in San Francisco and 7pm in Jerusalem...   *...do you know where they are?*

CN Tower

facts & statistics

- The tower measures 1,815 feet (553m) to the top of its antenna, and took more than three years to build.

- At a height of 1,151 feet (351m) there is a restaurant, called 360 The Restaurant, which revolves slowly for the best panoramic views.

- The observation gallery at 1,465 feet (447m) and known as the SkyPod, is the highest such structure in the world, allowing for fabulous views over the city and up to 100 miles (160km) beyond.

- Six elevators on the outside of the tower whisk visitors up and down at a speed of around 20 feet (6m) per second—a rate of ascent similar to that of a jet airplane.

- The CN Tower might have looked very different—in the early days, the proposal was for three towers linked together by bridges. This scheme was abandoned as impractical, and the single needle shape took form.

planning & construction

- Before work started on the Tower in 1973, members of the planning team toured the world on a fact-finding mission, so that they could plan not only the biggest, but also the best observation tower the world had seen.

- The design and build of the tower relied on teamwork to share expertise and push forward the barriers of knowledge. For this reason, no single architect or engineer is credited with its design.

- Psychologists were brought in to advise on the glass-fronted elevator design, to ensure that passengers would feel safe.

- At the level of the SkyPod it is sometimes possible to feel the whole Tower move slightly, as it flexes in a high wind—an essential requirement in its construction.

▶ TORONTO'S CN (CANADIAN NATIONAL) TOWER IS AN ICON OF CANADA, AND STILL HOLDS THE RECORD FOR THE WORLD'S TALLEST FREE-STANDING STRUCTURE.

did **you** know?

...it's here?

Canada

? Around 2 million people visit the CN Tower each year.

Q Can you guess the weight of this concrete and steel tower?

A It is calculated at 130,000 tons.

143

- At midday at the CN Tower it is 6pm in Ljubljana and 7pm on the River Nile...   ...do you know where they are?

Niagara Falls

USA

USA

> A FABULOUS DOUBLE WATERFALL SPANS THE BORDER BETWEEN CANADA AND THE UNITED STATES, AND AT NIGHT IS TRANSFORMED INTO A FLOODLIT MASTERPIECE.

did **you** know?

...it's here?

TIME ZONE: NIAGARA FALLS GMT-5

Q What is the outcrop of rock that separates the two sections of falls called?

A Goat Island

▸ When it is midday at Niagara Falls it is 8am in Anchorage and 11am at Chichén Itzá... ...do you know where they are?

? The American Falls stretch out in a straight line about 1,000 feet (305m) long, and tumble onto piles of rocks at their base.

TIME ZONE: NIAGARA FALLS GMT-5

dolomite &
sandstone

- Niagara Falls is a recent phenomenon in geological terms at around 10,000 years old.

- The river bedrock above the falls is hard dolomite, but underneath lie layers of softer rocks such as shale and sandstone, exposed below the falls by the fast-flowing river.

- People have defied death by going over the falls in barrels, boats, and sealed capsules. In 1859 Charles Blondin famously crossed over the waterfalls on a tightrope.

Lake Erie &
Lake Ontario

- The falls are located on the Niagara River, which flows out of Lake Erie and into Lake Ontario, 35 miles (56km) away.

- The sheer 165 feet (50m) drop and narrow arc of the Horseshoe Falls, 2,600 feet (792m) long, form the Canadian side.

? The best way to see Niagara Falls is from the little passenger boat, *Maid of the Mist*, which carries you right into the spray at the base of the waterfalls.

Lincoln Memorial

> ON FEBRUARY 12 EACH YEAR A
> BIRTHDAY WREATH IS PLACED
> ON THIS TRULY SPECTACULAR
> WASHINGTON MONUMENT, IN
> MEMORY OF ONE OF AMERICA'S
> GREAT LEADERS.

did **you** know?

...it's here?

rugged &
monumental

- The memorial is in the style of a classical Greek temple and in fact, looks very much like the Acropolis in Athens may have done in its heyday. It is dedicated to Abraham Lincoln (1809–65), the 16th US president, noted for his qualities of tolerance, honesty, and constancy.

- Lincoln rose to power as a leading orator in the anti-slavery movement, and presided over a divided America during its Civil War, finally uniting the country.

- Lincoln was shot by a deranged actor, John Wilkes Booth, while he was enjoying a visit to a theater in Washington, and died the next morning. Lincoln was an upright, upstanding figure of a man who would be greatly mourned.

heroic &
dedicated

- It took until 1922 to complete the memorial in Lincoln's honor, and it was the design of architect Henry Bacon—who was heavily influenced by classical Greek style, and created an imposing temple, complete with 38 Doric columns.

- Inside the building is a colossal, rugged statue of Lincoln carved from blocks of marble that have been fitted together so well that the joints are practically invisible. President Lincoln is depicted sitting in a massive chair.

- Tributes within the memorial include the words of his famous Gettysburg Address of 1863, carved in stone.

➤ *At midday at the Lincoln Memorial it is 1pm in Santo Domingo and 6pm at St. Peter's Basilica...*   *...do you know where they are?*

Statue of Liberty

symbolic &
colossal

- The Statue of Liberty is 151 feet (46m) high, and stands on a large stone plinth which is itself 154 feet (47m) high.

- It was presented to the American people as a gift of approval from the Old World by the French, and designed by the noted sculptor Frédéric Auguste Bartholdi. He had the benefit of Gustav Eiffel's engineering skills (creator of the Eiffel Tower in Paris).

- Bartholdi modeled the features of the statue on his own mother's face.

- The statue was first assembled in Paris, for its presentation to the American ambassador. It was then dismantled and then shipped to the site in New York harbor where it was put back together in its new permanent home.

- A spiral staircase inside the statue gives access to the seven-spiked crown, where windows look out over the harbor. It has been closed to the public in recent years, due to fears that it might become a terrorist target.

> ➤ THE STATUE OF LIBERTY, SYMBOL OF NEW YORK, OF FREEDOM, AND OF OPPORTUNITY IN A NEW WORLD, HAS BEEN GREETING IMMIGRANTS TO THE USA SINCE 1886.

did **you** know?

...it's here?

Statue of Liberty *USA*

▶ *At midday at the Statue of Liberty it is 7pm in Bucharest and 11.30pm at the Taj Mahal…*   *…do you know where they are?*

Empire State Building

> ▶ FOR 40 YEARS NEW YORK'S EMPIRE STATE BUILDING WAS THE TALLEST SKYSCRAPER IN THE WORLD, AND HELD ITS RECORD PROUDLY.

art deco &
stylish

● In a modern age of ever-taller towers of glass, concrete, and steel, it is all too easy to forget the impact of the Empire State Building, which held the record for the world's tallest skyscraper between 1931 and 1971. It may now be dwarfed by its taller neighbors, but it is still a potent symbol of the excitement and novelty of this exuberant city.

● Its total height is 1,472 feet (449m), including the television tower (added in 1985, and 22 floors high in its own right), so it is small wonder that its creators imagined mooring airships to the top. It was a glamorous idea that was soon rejected as impractical.

● The cost of the building was $41 million, a figure well below the original estimate.

● The Empire State Building has 102 floors, and every year a race is held to see who can race up the 1,576 stairs to the observation deck on the 86th floor in the fastest time—the current record is just under ten breathless minutes.

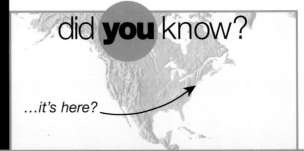

did **you** know?

...it's here?

EMPIRE STATE

Empire State Building *USA*

Q *In which famous movie did a monster gorilla try to climb the Empire State Building?*

A King Kong.

▶ *At midday at the Empire State Building it is 1am in Taipei and 7pm at the Blue Mosque...* *...do you know where they are?*

Inca Trails

▶ AN ANCIENT SYSTEM OF TRACKS WINDS THROUGH THE HIGH ANDES MOUNTAINS OF PERU AND BOLIVIA, GIVING A GLIMPSE OF THE GREAT INCA EMPIRE WHICH RULED HERE.

did **you** know?

...they are here?

Bolivia

long &
winding

- Like the Romans in Europe, the Incas of South America were great road builders—but where the Romans built in straight lines, the Incas were forced to zigzag their trails high into and over the Andes mountains.

- The Inca Empire had about 25,000 miles (40,250km) of roads in total, which varied from narrow tracks barely wide enough for a walker or a beast, to comparatively generous, broad roads where the terrain permitted.

- The network of roads led from the Amazon basin in the east to the coastal plain in the west of the continent, and from Argentina in the south to what is now Colombia in the north.

- All Inca roads led ultimately to the capital, Cuzco, from where relay teams of fleet-footed messengers could be dispatched at will.

- The Takesi Inca Trail in Bolivia, is the best preserved stretch of paved Inca route. It is 25 miles (40km) long and runs from mountains to jungle in the course of a couple of days.

- The most popular stretch for walkers today is the Inca Trail in Peru that leads from the ancient Inca capital of Cuzco, up the mountain flank of Machu Picchu to explore the mysterious rediscovered settlement at the top.

 The Inca Trail to Machu Picchu is protected as a UNESCO World Heritage Site. All development, such as facilities for tourists, is prohibited.

Iguassu Falls

► PROBABLY THE MOST SPECTACULAR WATERFALLS IN THE WORLD, THE VAST HORSESHOE-SHAPED IGUASSU FALLS STRADDLE THE BORDER OF ARGENTINA AND BRAZIL.

did **you** know?

...they are here?

Brasil/Argentina

dramatic &
forceful

- The Iguassu Falls mark a drop of about 270 feet (82m) in the River Iguassu, at a point where the waters have broadened out to 2.5 miles (4km).

- The river rises in the Serro do Mar, close to the coast of Brazil just south of São Paulo, and travels westward inland for 820 miles (1,320km) before reaching this point.

- The Iguassu Falls are at the edge of the Paraná Plateau, with 70 smaller waterfalls upstream as the waters gather force.

- The falls consist of as many as 275 separate cascades, which either plunge directly downward into the foam beneath, or first tumble over rocky outcrops.

- The sheer scale of the waterfalls means that the area is permanently cloaked with a fine mist of spray. Rocks between the cascades are covered in trees and a dense foliage of palms and ferns, while colorful wildflowers including begonias, bromeliads, and beautiful orchids shelter in the undergrowth.

- National parks in both Argentina and Brazil flank the Iguassu Falls. Walkways extend out over the river allowing visitors breathtaking, close-up views.

➤ *At midday at the Iguassu Falls it is 9am in Guatemala and 10am at Machu Picchu…*   *…do you know where they are?*

Index

Acknowledgments

Abbreviations for terms appearing below: (t) top; (b) bottom; (c) center; (l) left; (r) right; (AA) AA World Travel Library.

The Automobile Association wishes to thank the following photographers and companies for their assistance in the preparation of this book.

3 AA/E Meacher; 4c AA/E Meacher; 4r AA/J F Pins; 5tl AA/M Chaplow; 5tcl AA/A Baker; 5tc AA/C Sawyer; 5tcr AA/T Harris; 5tr AA/D Corrance; 5cl AA/R Strange; 5clc AA/R Ireland; 5crc AA/A Belcher; 5cr AA/P Kenward; 8 AA/J Loader; 10/1 AA/C Coe; 11l AA/C Coe; 11r AA/G Munday; 12 AA/K Paterson; 12/3 AA/J Beazley; 13 AA/J Smith; 14/5 AA/E Meacher; 15 AA/E Meacher; 16/7 AA/I Burgum; 17tr AA/I Burgum; 17c AA/I Burgum; 17bc AA/I Burgum; 18/9 AA/I Burgum; 19tr AA/S Day; 19c AA/I Burgum; 19bc AA/I Burgum; 20 AA/S Day; 21cl AA/S Day; 21tr AA/S Day; 21c AA/S Day; 21b AA/S Day; 22 AA/S Day; 22/3 AA/M Chaplow; 23 AA/S Day; 24 AA/P Wilson; 25l AA/S Day; 25r AA/S Day; 26 AA/J Edmanson; 27l AA/D Robertson; 27r AA/D Robertson; 28/9 AA/J Tims; 29tr AA/B Rieger; 29bc AA/P Enticknap; 30 AA/D Noble; 31t AA/D Noble; 31b AA/ D Noble; 32/3 AA/B Smith; 33 AA/A Baker; 35l AA/A Kouprianoff; 35r AA/A Kouprianoff; 36/7 AA/S Day; 37 AA/S Day; 38/9 AA/A Baker; 39t AA/A Baker; 39b Katey Mackenzie; 40tl AA/C Sawyer; 40bl AA/A Mockford & N Bonetti; 41l AA/A Mockford & N Bonetti; 41r AA/A Mockford & N Bonetti; 42/3 AA/C Sawyer; 43 AA/C Sawyer; 44 AA/A Kouprianoff; 45t AA/D Mitidieri; 45b AA/A Kouprianoff; 46 AA/A Kouprianoff; 47t AA/S McBride; 47b AA/S McBride; 48l AA/M Siebert; 48r AA/M Siebert; 49tr AA/J Smith; 49l AA/J Smith; 50 AA/S McBride; 51l AA/S McBride; 51tr AA/S McBride; 52/3 Romanian National Tourist Office UK & Ireland; 54/5 AA/R Surman; 55 AA/T Harris; 56/7 AA/T Harris; 57 AA/R Surman; 58/9 AA/C Sawyer; 59t AA/C Sawyer; 59b AA/M Birkitt; 60/1 AA/P Bennett; 61 AA/P Kenward; 62 AA/C Sawyer; 63l AA/C Sawyer; 63r AA/T Souter; 65l AA/P Kenward; 65r AA/P Kenward; 66 AA/R Strange; 67tr AA/C Coe; 67ct AA/R Strange; 67c AA/R Strange; 67cb AA/R Strange; 68/9 AA/R Strange; 69 AA/R Strange; 70/1 AA/C Coe; 71tc Kat Mead; 71tr AA/C Coe; 71bc Kat Mead; 72 AA/C Coe; 72tr AA/C Coe; 73c Kat Mead; 73bc AA/ R Strange; 74/5 AA/P Aithie; 75tr AA/J Loader; 75c AA/ P Aithie; 75bc AA/T Souter; 76 AA/J Loader; 77l AA/P Aithie; 77r AA/J Loader; 78 AA/J Loader; 79tr AA/J Loader; 79bc AA/J Loader; 80 AA/K Paterson; 81l AA/K Paterson; 81r AA/K Paterson; 82/3 AA/K Paterson; 83t AA/K Paterson; 83b AA/K Paterson; 84/5 AA/P Kenward; 85tr AA/E Meacher; 85bl AA/P Kenward; 85bc AA/P Kenward; 85br AA/P Kenward; 86t AA/P Kenward; 86b AA/P Kenward; 86/7 AA/P Kenward; 87 AA/E Meacher; 88 AA/J Gocher; 89tr AA/S Watkins; 89tc AA/J Gocher; 89c AA/J Gocher; 89bc AA/S Watkins; 91l AA/D Corrance; 91r AA/D Corrance; 92/3 AA/D Corrance; 93 AA/D Corrance; 94 AA/R Strange; 95l AA/R Strange; 95r AA/R Strange; 96/7 AA/R Strange; 97tr AA/D Henley; 97c AA/D Henley; 97bc AA/R Strange; 98 AA/I Morejohn; 99t AA/L K Stow; 99c AA/L K Stow; 99b AA/L K Stow; 100/1 AA/G Clements; 101 AA/I Morejohn; 102l AA/I Morejohn; 102r AA/I Morejohn; 103l AA/G Clements; 103r AA/G Clements; 104 AA/D Buwalda; 105t AA/B Davies; 105b AA/D Buwalda; 106 AA/J Holmes; 107l AA/D Corrance; 107r AA/J Holmes; 108/9 AA/A Baker; 109 AA/Baker; 110 AA/P Kenward; 111l AA/P Kenward; 111c AA/S Day; 111r AA/S Day; 112 Tourism Queensland; 113tr ATC; 113cl Tourism Queensland; 113b Tourism Queensland; 114 AA/A Belcher; 115tr AA/M Langford; 115cl AA/Belcher; 115c AA/M Langford; 116/7 AA/P Kenward; 117 AA/P Kenward; 118 AA/M Langford; 118/9 AA/A Belcher; 119tc AA/A Belcher; 119tr AA/P Kenward; 120/1 AA/K L Alder; 121 AA/K L Alder; 122 AA/K Paterson; 123l AA/K Paterson; 123r AA/K Paterson; 124/5 AA/R Ireland; 125t AA/K Paterson; 125b AA/K Paterson; 126/7 AA/R Ireland; 127 AA/R Ireland; 128/9 AA/M van Vark; 129 AA/M van Vark; 130/1 AA/M van Vark; 132/3 AA/M van Vark; 134t AA/R Strange; 134b AA/R Strange; 135l AA/R Strange; 135r AA/R Strange; 136 AA/R Strange; 137l AA/R Strange; 137c AA/R Strange; 137r AA/R Strange; 138/9 AA/G Marks; 139l AA/G Marks; 139c AA/G Marks; 139r AA/G Marks; 140/1 AA/G Marks; 141 AA/G Marks; 142/3 AA/J F Pins; 143 AA/N Sumner; 144/5 AA/J F Pins; 145 AA/N Sumner; 146/7tl AA/N Sumner; 148/9 AA/C Sawyer; 150/1 AA/C Sawyer; 151 AA/E Rooney; 152 AA/S McBride; 153l AA/D Corrance; 153r AA/S McBride; 154 AA/G Marks; 155t AA/G Marks; 155b AA/G Marks; 156/7 www.IguassuFallsTour.com.

Every effort has been made to trace the copyright holders, and we apologise in advance for any accidental errors. We would be happy to apply the corrections in the following edition of this publication.